"In a world that encourages an 'all about me' mentality, I am so grateful for this devotional that helps us learn all about Him. Let the words on these pages refresh you as you reflect on our great and loving God."

Esther Fleece Allen, bestselling author of *No More Faking Fine* and *Your New Name*

"Tara-Leigh Cobble's masterful and fresh way of revealing the nuances and meaning of Scripture is nothing short of inspiring. In her latest work, she offers bite-sized wisdom that is like a jolt of spiritual insight that will ignite your passion for learning more about God and being more of who He has called you to be."

Valorie Burton, CEO of The CaPP Institute

"I am so thankful for this devotional that reveals God's character and love in the most encouraging and understandable way. These snapshots of His attributes and goodness keep me encouraged and in tune with God throughout the day."

Lauren Scruggs Kennedy, wellness expert, author, and entrepreneur

"Tara-Leigh has done it again. A perfect balance of theology and practicality. Her whimsical, daily approach to experiencing the Scriptures draws me into the larger unified story of the Bible. A wonderful daily companion."

Michael Dean McDonald, chief global focus officer for BibleProject

"You'd be hard-pressed to find someone more capable than TLC to explain Scripture in a way that's meaningful, impactful, and relevant for today. I've grown so much in my faith journey because of her Spirit-inspired work!"

Paula Faris, journalist, founder of CARRY Media™, and author

"With fist-pounding passion and clarity, this devotional will nail the truth of God's love to your heart. I urge you to listen up. A new way of life is possible—starting now!"

Rashawn Copeland, founder of Blessed Media and author of *Start Where You Are* and *No Turning Back*

"Tara-Leigh has taken the time to dive deep into the depths of God's Word and draw out nuggets of wisdom. The insight she shares brings joyful understanding of the riches of God's character."

Lauren Green McAfee, corporate ambassador for Hobby Lobby and author of *Only One Life* and *Not What You Think*

"*'He's where the joy is.'* This statement is an engine that drives the purpose for which we were all made. Tara-Leigh Cobble not only expounds upon this concept through *The God Shot*, but she authentically embodies it in her own life. This book is fuel for the engine of your joy in God!"

Lee McDerment, pastor of prayer, prophecy, and preaching at NewSpring Church

"*The God Shot* is a blessing to our listeners on KSBJ Houston and the WayFM network. Hearing Tara-Leigh on the air with related content shows how gifted, yet approachable, she is at teaching God's Word. These printed glimpses of His character are wonderful reminders that 'He's where the joy is.'"

Tim Dukes, chief operating officer of Hope Media Group

"Tara-Leigh Cobble has a gift for communicating timeless biblical truths in a timely method, and this book is a perfect example. *The God Shot* gives you a handle on a better understanding of God's character—taking truths that are eternally valuable and making them immediately practical."

Brad Cooper, lead pastor of NewSpring Church

THE
GOD
SHOT

ALSO BY TARA-LEIGH COBBLE

The Bible Recap

The Bible Recap Deluxe Edition

The Bible Recap Study Guide

The Bible Recap Journal

He's Where the Joy Is

He's Where the Joy Is, Teen Edition

THE GOD SHOT

100 SNAPSHOTS OF GOD'S CHARACTER IN SCRIPTURE

TARA-LEIGH COBBLE

BETHANYHOUSE
a division of Baker Publishing Group
Minneapolis, Minnesota

Published by Bethany House Publishers
11400 Hampshire Avenue South
Minneapolis, Minnesota 55438
www.bethanyhouse.com

Bethany House Publishers is a division of
Baker Publishing Group, Grand Rapids, Michigan

Printed in the United States of America

Library of Congress Cataloging-in-Publication Data
Names: Cobble, Tara-Leigh, author.
Title: The God shot : 100 snapshots of God's character in scripture / Tara-Leigh Cobble.
Description: Minneapolis, Minnesota : Bethany House Publishers, a division of Baker
    Publishing Group, [2022]
Identifiers: LCCN 2022008629 | ISBN 9780764240331 (cloth) | ISBN 9781493439195
    (ebook)
Subjects: LCSH: God—Biblical teaching. | Bible—Meditations.
Classification: LCC BT103 .C63 2022 | DDC 231—dc23/eng/20220325
LC record available at https://lccn.loc.gov/2022008629

These devotional readings were adapted
from The God Shot radio features by Tara-
Leigh Cobble, first aired in 2020.

Cover design by Rob Williams, InsideOut
Creative Arts, Inc.

The author is represented by Alive Literary
Agency, www.aliveliterary.com.

Baker Publishing Group publications use
paper produced from sustainable forestry
practices and post-consumer waste whenever possible.

22   23   24   25   26   27   28   7   6   5   4   3   2   1

**This book is dedicated to
Eva Royer.**

Your zeal and passion for this project
have been far more impactful than we ever imagined!
I'm so grateful for you and your friendship, wisdom,
and hard work to make this happen!

CONTENTS

About This Book

The God Shot devotional explores small, powerful sections from each book of the New Testament one day at a time. By reading the passages in context, you'll be able to see the meaning of each individual verse in new ways and how they tie together to weave a picture of God and His goodness.

Each day's reading points toward a name or attribute of God that the passage reveals, showing how God's character can be found throughout Scripture. In these quick and helpful "snapshots" directly focused on the Word of God, you'll not only be encouraged, but you'll learn more about who God is and how to find Him on every page of the Bible.

It's a Bible study in ninety seconds or less—but even in its brevity, my hope is that you'll find it dense with theological truth and encouragement.

THE GOD OF PEACE

MATTHEW 6:25-33

DAY 1

Therefore I tell you, do not be anxious about your life, what you will eat or what you will drink, nor about your body, what you will put on. Is not life more than food, and the body more than clothing?

MATTHEW 6:25

These words fall in the middle of Jesus's most famous sermon, the Sermon on the Mount. The verse opens with "therefore," which means Jesus is making a connection between the specific truth He mentioned in the previous verses and why it's important for us not to be anxious about our life. In the verses prior to this, He says it's because this life isn't where our focus should be. And you can't worry about something you aren't focused on.

Instead, Jesus says we should aim to focus on our true home, which is in the next life—in God's kingdom. The things that cause us anxiety are often things that are "passing away" (1 John 2:17), but Jesus wants us to focus on the things that will last.

Are you anxious over temporary things? What is disrupting your peace today? Where do you feel like God has forgotten you? Talk to Him about it. He can be trusted, and His trustworthiness is the only thing that can truly set your heart at peace. He's where the joy is!

DAY 2

Look at the birds of the air: they neither sow nor reap nor gather into barns, and yet your heavenly Father feeds them. Are you not of more value than they? And which of you by being anxious can add a single hour to his span of life?

MATTHEW 6:26–27

When Jesus preaches the Sermon on the Mount, His audience is probably filled with farmers and fishermen and shepherds, so He uses imagery they can easily understand. For instance, He references birds. He says they live a good life off what God provides for them. And if God is attentive even to birds, how much more attention does He pay to His kids?

We're given to anxiety when we forget that God is attentive and active in our lives, so Jesus reminds them. He doesn't want them to be anxious. This is a common theme throughout Scripture. In fact, 366 times in Scripture God tells His kids not to be afraid—once for every day of the year, including leap years. I think it's interesting that God never gives that counsel to His enemies; He only gives it to His kids. Why? Because fathers provide for their own children. God your Father is providing for *you* today.

Is your heart at peace right now? Or does it need to remember the goodness of your Father's attentive love? If you're feeling anxious, be on the lookout today for all the ways your Father has provided and is providing for you. He's where the joy is!

DAY 3

Why are you anxious about clothing? Consider the lilies of the field, how they grow: they neither toil nor spin, yet I tell you, even Solomon in all his glory was not arrayed like one of these.

MATTHEW 6:28–29

Today, Jesus continues speaking in the Sermon on the Mount. He's talking to His followers, many of whom are everyday people living in an agrarian society. The poorer people in the crowd probably have legitimate concerns about how they'll put food on the table or clothes on their kids' backs. Whereas the wealthier disciples may be concerned not with *having* clothes, but with having *the best* clothes.

Like them, some of us may be concerned about being clothed, but the majority of us are probably more concerned about having the kinds of clothes that will help us feel admired or desired. Either way, Jesus says it's foolish to put our focus on clothes to this degree. One of the sad things about the human heart is that we like to carve out new pits to fill with anxiety even when there's no legitimate need.

God is your provider. He knows all your needs. He is attentive to them. That means you have enough for this moment. And the next. And the next. Are there places where you've forgotten this? Thank Him for meeting your needs in the past. Ask Him to meet your needs in the present. Trust Him to meet your needs in the future. Rest in the peace of His provision. He's where the joy is!

DAY 4

If God so clothes the grass of the field, which today is alive and tomorrow is thrown into the oven, will he not much more clothe you, O you of little faith?

MATTHEW 6:30

Jesus and His followers are sitting on one of the rolling green hills along the Sea of Galilee. As He continues His Sermon on the Mount, He makes a grand statement about the Father's provision, and He uses the landscape as evidence. I imagine Him sweeping His arm across the field and saying, "Look, you guys! See this grass? God pays attention to every blade of it, every tiny slice of His creation, so don't doubt for a second that He's paying attention to you!" He keeps reminding them of the Father's character—that He can be trusted. He aims to set their hearts at peace.

Then Jesus invents a word. It shows up five times in Scripture but nowhere else outside of Scripture. It basically translates to "little-faiths," and it reads kind of like a term of endearment. *Oh, little-faiths, your Father is so much better than you know. Trust Him.*

Do you feel like a "little-faith" today? If so, there's good news for you: Jesus didn't condemn those of little faith. He leaned in to encourage them. Today, pray the prayer of Mark 9:24, "I believe; help my unbelief!" He stands ready to help you, to equip you with faith. He's where the joy is!

DAY 5

Therefore do not be anxious, saying, "What shall we eat?" or "What shall we drink?" or "What shall we wear?" For the Gentiles seek after all these things, and your heavenly Father knows that you need them all. Seek first the kingdom of God and his righteousness, and all these things will be added to you.

MATTHEW 6:31–33

There are lots of things in life we can be anxious about, and they seem to increase every day. We have new things to be afraid of that never would've crossed the minds of our ancestors. Most of them probably fall under the heading of "fleeting things," but *all* of them fall under "things that our under our loving Father's control."

As we've learned, Jesus's early followers were mostly poor and likely had real concerns about food and clothing. But Jesus keeps reminding them that their Father will provide for them in every need. No area of their life is beyond His care.

If you feel anxious, ask yourself what you're chasing. If you're chasing temporary things, you'll always crave more. And your anxiety will increase as you watch life slip through your fingers. Jesus tells His followers to prioritize things of eternal value because God will handle the big deals *and* the details. He wants to set their hearts at peace by reminding them that God can be trusted.

Are you prioritizing God's kingdom? Are you seeking His righteousness? If not, how can you align your heart with His priorities today? Ask Him to help you. He's where the joy is!

THE GOD OF COMPASSION

DAY 6

> When [Jesus] went ashore he saw a great crowd, and he had compassion on them, because they were like sheep without a shepherd. And he began to teach them many things.
>
> **MARK 6:34**

When this passage opens, Jesus has just gotten the news that His cousin, John the Baptist, who was the forerunner of His ministry, has been beheaded in prison. It's heavy news. In the verses right before this, it seems clear that Jesus is trying to get some alone time, but people just keep needing things from Him. They follow Him everywhere He goes, expecting more from Him.

Have you ever felt like this—like you're already being crushed by the weight of life, and then even more demands come your way? Jesus knows how that feels. And do you know how He responds? With compassion. He shows empathy. He sees their neediness, and He enters in, patiently teaching the wayward and providing for the needy. By the way, that's us too. We're wayward. We're needy. And He always has time for us.

Where do you feel needy today? Where do the demands of life feel like they're too much for you? Jesus, your Good Shepherd, draws near to show you compassion. Receive what He gives. Learn from what He teaches you today. He's where the joy is!

DAY 7

When it grew late, his disciples came to him and said, "This is a desolate place, and the hour is now late. Send them away to go into the surrounding countryside and villages and buy themselves something to eat." But he answered them, "You give them something to eat."

MARK 6:35–37

After John the Baptist is beheaded in prison, Jesus tries to get some time alone—perhaps to mourn—but instead, a crowd of thousands follows Him. Despite the loss He's suffered, Jesus has compassion on the crowd and leans in to meet their needs.

After He teaches for a while, the disciples are ready to pack up and call it a night—especially because it's time for dinner and they don't have food. But Jesus suggests they do even more work; He tells the disciples they're on kitchen duty. Where, exactly, will they get all this food to feed thousands? We'll find out more in the days ahead, but there's still something we can discover about God in today's verses, and it's likely what the disciples learned in this moment too: His compassion exceeds what seems normal, and His provision exceeds what seems possible.

Do you ever feel like a burden to God? Does what you want or need seem impossible? He's the perfect place to take all your desires, because not only does He always have enough of everything, but He also has a heart that is guided by compassion. Tell Him your wants—even the things that seem impossible—and trust that He'll always do what's best. He's where the joy is!

DAY 8

They said to him, "Shall we go and buy two hundred denarii worth of bread and give it to them to eat?" And [Jesus] said to them, "How many loaves do you have? Go and see." And when they had found out, they said, "Five, and two fish." Then he commanded them all to sit down in groups on the green grass. So they sat down in groups, by hundreds and by fifties.

MARK 6:37–40

In this passage, Jesus has been teaching a crowd of thousands, but as the day unfolds, suddenly it's time for dinner, so the disciples want to send the people home. Jesus, on the other hand, wants to feed the crowd.

There's one major problem, though; the disciples point out that they don't have enough money. They apparently only have two hundred denarii among them, which is roughly the amount a day laborer makes in six months. Some scholars say this was the money they'd set aside for their small crew to live off as they traveled with Jesus. It certainly wasn't enough to feed the crowd, and even if it would cover that expense, the disciples would be bankrupt afterward.

But God not only has an abundant supply, He has an *ordered plan*. Tomorrow we'll read more about His provision, but as for today, the five loaves and two fish seem insufficient, don't they?

What needs do you feel insufficient to meet today? Where does God's provision seem lacking to you? Wait to see how He proves Himself good and compassionate in your situation. Look for it. Trust that He will. He's where the joy is!

DAY 9

Taking the five loaves and the two fish, he looked up to heaven and said a blessing and broke the loaves and gave them to the disciples to set before the people. And he divided the two fish among them all. And they all ate and were satisfied. And they took up twelve baskets full of broken pieces and of the fish. And those who ate the loaves were five thousand men.

MARK 6:41–44

We've been reading about one of Jesus's most well-known miracles, feeding thousands. Scripture records five thousand men, but when you count women and children, there were likely around fifteen thousand present. That's a *lot* of food.

While this food may seem like something the people need, it's probably more of a *want*—most people wouldn't die of starvation from skipping one meal. Despite the apparent lack of severity, Jesus leans in with compassion. He takes these seven little things and multiplies them so that everyone in the immediate area is blessed.

The gospel of John says the five loaves and two fish come from a boy in the crowd. On his own, the boy doesn't have enough to feed all the people, but God uses what the boy offers and *makes it* enough. Likewise, Scripture never says *we* are enough. In fact, it repeatedly says we aren't. But God is enough, and He uses the little we have in ways we could never imagine.

What "little" has He given you to offer back to Him today? You never know how He might multiply it or use it to bless those around you by demonstrating His compassion. He's where the joy is!

THE GOD WHO LOVES CONVERSATION

DAY 10

Now Jesus was praying in a certain place, and when he finished, one of his disciples said to him, "Lord, teach us to pray, as John taught his disciples."

LUKE 11:1

Prayer is a conversation with God. It may seem that since Jesus is God, there'd be no reason for Him to pray, but throughout Scripture, we see Him talking to the Father. He shows us that oneness is about constant communication. Scripture says to pray without ceasing—to have a lifestyle of prayer. And Jesus demonstrates that.

When the disciples see Jesus talking to the Father, they see something beautiful and desirable, and they want it for themselves. They say, "Teach us how to do that!" So if you feel awkward or insecure about your prayers, the good news is it's a skill you can learn! And Jesus teaches us how to do it. He wants us to have relational intimacy with the Father because God loves to talk to His kids!

Do you struggle to pray? Ever wonder if you're "doing it right"? Or maybe you don't pray often because you don't want to bother God? He invites you to talk to Him. He wants to hear from you. He's never too busy. Today, aim to talk to Him about everything—from your daily bread to your deep desires. He wants to hear it all, so lean in and tell Him! He's where the joy is!

DAY 11

He said to them, "When you pray, say: 'Father, hallowed be your name. Your kingdom come. Give us each day our daily bread.'"

LUKE 11:2–3

In today's verse, Jesus is teaching His disciples how to pray. They've seen Him talk to the Father, and they want to be able to have those conversations with the Father too.

First, Jesus shows that prayer begins with relationship. If you've been adopted into God's family, then you're God's child and you can call Him Father. He's the best Father—one who fills in all the gaps and aches left by earthly fathers.

Next, Jesus recognizes the Father's holiness and prioritizes His kingdom. By acknowledging all those things first—that we're His kids and He's to be set apart and honored above all—it helps us remember to be openhanded about the things we ask Him for. Not only does God provide for the daily needs of His kids, but beyond that, Scripture says all good gifts come from God. He's a giver!

Do your prayers lack any of these elements? Do you know God as Father and trust His heart toward you?

Do you honor His name? Do you prioritize His kingdom? Do you ask Him for what you want and need? Today, draw near. Tell Him. He loves to hear from you, and He's where the joy is!

DAY 12

> Forgive us our sins, for we ourselves forgive everyone who is indebted to us. And lead us not into temptation.*
>
> **LUKE 11:4**

*Matthew's account of the Lord's Prayer includes the phrase "but deliver us from evil."

After overhearing Jesus's conversations with the Father, His disciples ask Him how they can have that kind of intimacy for themselves.

When Jesus first started to guide them through prayer (11:2), He opened by pointing to their relationship with the Father—His holiness, His kingdom, His provision— and here Jesus mentions other things that come up in all relationships—sin and forgiveness. As long as we're alive, our relationship with the Father will include our sins and His forgiveness. But those sins no longer act as a barrier between us and the Father, because Jesus absorbed all the Father's wrath for our sins. We don't have to fear His wrath. He invites us to confess our sins to Him.

Finally, He also prompts us to ask for help against future sins. God cares deeply about our hearts and wants us to avoid the sins and trials that lead us astray.

Do you confess your sins to God? Do you trust His forgiveness toward you? Do you ask for His help to keep from falling into sin? May He guide you away from temptation and into the joy of intimacy with Him, because He's where the joy is!

THE GOD OF LIGHT AND TRUTH

DAY 13

In the beginning was the Word, and the Word was with God, and the Word was God. He was in the beginning with God.

JOHN 1:1–2

The apostle John, one of Jesus's inner circle, wrote this gospel and a few other books in the Bible. His writings consistently point to the theme that Jesus is God.

Jesus has many names that serve to reveal His character and His actions; one of His names is "the Word." In these verses, John lets us know that the Word has always existed, even before He was born in Bethlehem. He wasn't created by the Father.

The three persons of the Trinity—Father, Son, and Spirit—are eternally united and eternally distinct. When John says, "The Word was with God, and the Word was God," he shows us the unity and distinction that exist within the Trinity. It can be challenging to try to understand the Trinity, but verses like this help us to see a little more about God—specifically, how relational He is by His very nature. He enters into relationship with us, shining His light and truth into our dark world.

In what dark corner of your life do you need the Word of truth to speak to you today? It's such a blessing that the triune God wants to be in relationship with us, because He's where the joy is!

DAY 14

All things were made through him, and without him was not any thing made that was made.

JOHN 1:3

The apostle John opens his letter by diving straight into the identity of Jesus. He calls Jesus "the Word," and he points out that not only was Jesus *not* created, but Jesus is the one who did the manual labor of creation. He has always existed, and everything else exists because of Him.

Paul reiterates this in Colossians 1:16: "By him all things were created, in heaven and on earth, visible and invisible, whether thrones or dominions or rulers or authorities—all things were created through him and for him." Even the Old Testament points to this. When God said, "Let us make man in our image, after our likeness" (Genesis 1:26), who is the "us"? Most scholars say this is a conversation among the Trinity—Father, Son, and Spirit.

Scripture repeatedly points to Jesus as the builder of creation. He made all of this, including you, for Himself. Your chief purpose in life is to reflect and connect with your Creator. Is there a space in your life where you feel disconnected from Him? Is there something He purposed in creating you that you're afraid to lean into? May the light and truth of His love for you draw you in. He's where the joy is!

DAY 15

In him was life, and the life was the light of men. The light shines in the darkness, and the darkness has not overcome it.

JOHN 1:4–5

In John's gospel, he lays his foundation by forming our understanding of who Jesus is. In the first three verses, John tells us that Jesus is God, is the Word of God, has always existed, and created everything. Today he points out that Jesus is the source of life and light.

Our fallen world is a dark place filled with broken people. It's hard to find our way and see the right path. Scripture says Jesus is the very light by which we see. Being in a relationship with Him and getting to know Him better has a way of making things clearer. The world offers you a thousand ways to empower and improve yourself—and most of them feel like burdens, don't they? They require you to fix and heal yourself. But Jesus is the one who has accomplished all you can't. He brings life. He turns the light on.

What feels dark and hopeless in your life? Maybe it's an uncertainty you're dwelling in. Maybe it's a sin pattern you can't seem to overcome. Maybe it's a challenging relationship. No matter what darkness you face today, it is no match for His light! He's where the joy is!

THE GOD OF RESURRECTION

ACTS 2:22–33

DAY 16

Jesus of Nazareth, a man attested to you by God with mighty works and wonders and signs that God did through him in your midst, as you yourselves know—this Jesus, delivered up according to the definite plan and foreknowledge of God, you crucified and killed by the hands of lawless men. God raised him up, loosing the pangs of death, because it was not possible for him to be held by it.

ACTS 2:22–24

In this section of Scripture, the apostle Peter is addressing the people of Jerusalem who had crucified Jesus just seven weeks earlier. Jesus walked on earth for forty days after His resurrection before He ascended to heaven. So roughly ten days before this sermon, the resurrected Jesus ascended, and the apostles were left to explain His message to the locals.

Peter starts out with the bad news: You killed Jesus. That's where all our stories start, because we were all born into sin and our sin cost Jesus His life. But death is not stronger than God. That's what undergirds our great hope, because all of us who are in Christ will someday die too—but then we'll be raised like He was, by the power of God.

Peter says this was God's plan all along—that Jesus would move through death and into eternal life so that we could do the same. This also gives us hope for all the spaces of our lives that currently feel like death. What areas of your life need His resurrection power? May your heart be encouraged by the truth that death doesn't have the final word. Jesus does. And He's where the joy is!

DAY 17

David says concerning him, "I saw the Lord always before me, for he is at my right hand that I may not be shaken; therefore my heart was glad, and my tongue rejoiced; my flesh also will dwell in hope. For you will not abandon my soul to Hades, or let your Holy One see corruption."

ACTS 2:25–27

Not long before Peter speaks these words to the people of Jerusalem, they had crucified Jesus and He had risen from the dead. As the locals wrestle with the fact that Jesus seems to be more than a mere human, Peter explains the reality of who Jesus is, tracing the evidence all the way back to the Old Testament.

Peter quotes King David, and they're all familiar with David's words because they're part of Scripture. This particular passage is from one of David's songs (Psalm 16:10). Peter connects the dots for them, revealing that Jesus is the Messiah-God whom David wrote about a thousand years earlier. Yes, David prophesied about Jesus a thousand years before Jesus was born on earth.

David also said Jesus brought him gladness and joy and hope. That's true for us too. David rejoices in his relationship with God. Have you done that lately? After you finish reading, spend a few moments praising Him for who He is and what He's done. Thank Him for the fact that He hasn't abandoned you to the grave either! He keeps you for eternity, and He's where the joy is!

DAY 18

"You have made known to me the paths of life; you will make me full of gladness with your presence." Brothers, I may say to you with confidence about the patriarch David that he both died and was buried, and his tomb is with us to this day. Being therefore a prophet, and knowing that God had sworn with an oath to him that he would set one of his descendants on his throne, he foresaw and spoke about the resurrection of the Christ, that he was not abandoned to Hades, nor did his flesh see corruption.

ACTS 2:28–31

Here, Peter begins by quoting the words of David to the Jewish members of his audience. David was prophesying about the coming Messiah, and Peter is letting his listeners know that Jesus is the Messiah whom David wrote about!

These Jews revere David—he was their greatest king up to that point. But now Peter is saying that there is a better king, an eternal king. After all, David died and did not rise from the dead. They still have his body in the tomb. But Jesus is a descendant of David, and David had prophesied about Him. Jesus is the one whose body wouldn't decay or be abandoned to the grave.

The words of David paint a picture of now and forever. Because of Jesus's finished work on the cross, we have access now to the kind of gladness that only comes from being in God's presence. And because of His death and resurrection, we have access to the path to true life—*eternal* life.

Where do you lack gladness today? Where does your heart need to be revived by the joy that comes from your eternal relationship with the risen King? Jesus is your eternal life, and He's where the joy is!

DAY 19

This Jesus God raised up, and of that we all are witnesses. Being therefore exalted at the right hand of God, and having received from the Father the promise of the Holy Spirit, he has poured out this that you yourselves are seeing and hearing.

ACTS 2:32–33

Approximately seven weeks after Jesus was crucified, Peter preaches to the Jews in Jerusalem, expounding on Jesus's death, resurrection, and ascension. As far as they're concerned, there's no human explanation for what they witnessed—a man beaten beyond recognition, stabbed and crucified, who was raised and healed three days later.

Peter says the only explanation is supernatural. God is the one who raised Jesus from the dead. Jesus walked on earth for forty days, eating food and touching people, proving He wasn't a ghost, then He ascended to heaven. But He didn't leave earth hopeless, without the presence of God—He sent His Spirit to be with believers as a guarantee of their resurrection yet to come (2 Corinthians 1:22), to guide them and speak the truth of His Word to them.

Believer, that means you are not alone. His Holy Spirit lives in you, to equip you and encourage you and guide you, to grant you repentance, to remind you of your identity as His child. Do you recognize His ongoing work in your life? Today, listen for the promptings of the Holy Spirit. He is with you, and He's where the joy is!

THE GOD WHO IS SOVEREIGN

ROMANS 8:28-34

DAY 20

> We know that for those who love God all things work together for good, for those who are called according to his purpose.
>
> **ROMANS 8:28**

The apostle Paul is writing a letter to the Christians in Rome—a wealthy, decadent city. Rome is the center of government, and its people worship false gods, including the Roman emperor. Since Christians refuse to worship the emperor, they're experiencing severe persecution—from imprisonment to being burned alive.

In the midst of these trials, Paul writes to encourage the Roman believers, reminding them that God is still in control. Paul doesn't say all things *are* good, but that God is big enough to use even the evil actions of cruel leaders in a way that is ultimately and eternally best for His kids. Despite their circumstances, God is at work and He can be trusted. This is a promise that extends not to all people, but to all followers of Christ—to those who love God, the ones God has called to Himself.

What circumstances tempt you to doubt God's activity in your life? Have there been times in the past when He surprised you by turning a struggle into a blessing? Ask Him to help you trust His sovereignty today. Whether your day is filled with the good, the bad, or the ugly, He's working for your joy. And He's where the joy is!

DAY 21

Those whom he foreknew he also predestined to be conformed to the image of his Son, in order that he might be the firstborn among many brothers. Those whom he predestined he also called, and those whom he called he also justified, and those whom he justified he also glorified.

ROMANS 8:29–30

Paul's letter to the Roman Christians comes at a time when they're enduring trials that are both discouraging and terrifying. He takes care to remind them that God is working out His very good plan through everything they're enduring.

All along, God has planned to adopt them into His family and conform them to the image of His Son, Jesus, who also suffered the persecution of Rome, even to the point of death. Jesus didn't deserve death. We do—it's the penalty we've earned for our sins. But Paul says God has justified and glorified us. He has declared us righteous, despite our unrighteousness.

Even before you were born, God was working out your eternal destiny, providing for you in ways both temporary and eternal. His relationship with you will never end. He is the one who started it, and He is the one who will sustain it. He is at work in every moment, and He always has been.

Are there any areas of your life right now where God seems absent? What about the past—were there any times when you felt He abandoned you? Talk to Him about it. Ask Him to show up! He's with you today, and He's where the joy is!

DAY 22

What then shall we say to these things? If God is for us, who can be against us? He who did not spare his own Son but gave him up for us all, how will he not also with him graciously give us all things?

ROMANS 8:31–32

As Paul writes to encourage the Christians living under Rome's persecution, He reminds them that God is their help in all things. He's already told them that God chose them, called them to Himself, declared them righteous despite their sin, and uses their trials to conform them to the image of His Son, Jesus. Now, he goes on to point out that their identity and their eternity are secure.

Your future is sealed and certain. Nothing can thwart God's plan to redeem you. No enemy—whether it's as big and powerful as Rome or as small as the sin pattern you keep stumbling into—can threaten His love for you. If God gave you something as valuable as Jesus, He certainly won't skimp on giving you everything else you need. He delights to give good gifts to His kids!

What do you need today? What enemies do you feel helpless to fight? He's the one who can provide for you. He's the one who can protect you. He's the sovereign King of the universe, and whatever you need today, He knows, and He's at work on your behalf. He's where the joy is!

DAY 23

Who shall bring any charge against God's elect? It is God who justifies. Who is to condemn? Christ Jesus is the one who died—more than that, who was raised—who is at the right hand of God, who indeed is interceding for us.

ROMANS 8:33–34

As Paul writes this letter to the Roman Christians, many of them are being tortured and imprisoned for worshipping Jesus instead of the Roman emperor. Some of them have probably had false charges brought against them. Legal trouble is a present reality for them, as is death.

Paul reminds them of the greater reality at hand: God has the final say about our identities. We all started out as God's enemies, but Paul says God chose us, as Christ followers, and called us to Himself. Even though we're sinners, He calls us saints. Even though we're guilty, our debt and our sentence have been paid in full by Jesus. No one can condemn us, because the sovereign God of the universe has already declared our future, and He has the last word!

Not only does God have the final word, but He also has the ongoing word—Paul says Jesus is praying for you. He's seated on His throne, talking to the Father on your behalf.

Where have you been wrongly accused or intentionally misunderstood? What false identities have you lived under? Take heart: Jesus prays for you. He knows, He sees, and He's at work on your behalf. He's where the joy is!

THE GOD OF LOVE

1 CORINTHIANS 13:1–11

If I speak in the tongues of men and of angels, but have not love, I am a noisy gong or a clanging cymbal.

1 CORINTHIANS 13:1

This famous passage about love is part of the apostle Paul's letter to the church at Corinth, which is steeped in sin and idolatry. Paul spends a good bit of time in his letter warning them about their sinful actions, but he also lets them know that good, moral behavior isn't at the heart of what God is after.

God doesn't only care about our actions—He also cares about what motivates those actions. And because *God's* motive is love, He wants His people to be motivated by love too! Otherwise, we can trick ourselves into thinking we're "good people" when we're actually selfish people who just want to look good to others or feel good about ourselves.

Think about it: When you make better choices than someone else, isn't it a little too easy to feel proud and arrogant? Paul says we're missing the point entirely when we act and think like that. On top of that, it's annoying—like a noisy gong or a clanging cymbal. Where do you see these kinds of loveless "good deeds" show up in your life?

Today, may God equip you to tap into and be motivated by the great love He poured out on you through Jesus. He's where the joy is!

DAY 25

And if I have prophetic powers, and understand all mysteries and all knowledge, and if I have all faith, so as to remove mountains, but have not love, I am nothing. If I give away all I have, and if I deliver up my body to be burned, but have not love, I gain nothing.

1 CORINTHIANS 13:2–3

The Corinthian Christians are zealous for the things of God, but they're missing the mark on understanding God's heart, so Paul spends a lot of time correcting them in his letters. He wants their zeal to be an *educated* zeal, connected to and motivated by the truth of who God is.

They want to perform miracles and have all the right answers. They want to do big, impressive acts to demonstrate God's power. Meanwhile, other Christians are facing persecution and even death. So while the Corinthians want more power, other Christians are losing all their power and being martyred. Paul points out that neither extreme matters if love for God and others isn't at the heart of it all.

For instance, Jesus performed powerful miracles, then died at the hands of His persecutors. He experienced both extremes, but He was always motivated by His love for the Father and His love for His people. He didn't point to His own glory, but to the Father's glory and our joy.

What are you seeking? What are you pointing toward? Whether you're in a position of power or you're experiencing loss, may love point you and others back to Jesus today! He's where the joy is!

DAY 26

Love is patient and kind; love does not envy or boast; it is not arrogant or rude. It does not insist on its own way; it is not irritable or resentful; it does not rejoice at wrongdoing, but rejoices with the truth. Love bears all things, believes all things, hopes all things, endures all things.

1 CORINTHIANS 13:4–7

Paul's letter to the church at Corinth includes these famous words you've probably heard at weddings. But as much as they may inform and encourage the bride and groom, they are primarily about God. This is who He is. God's love patiently bears with us in all our failings. God's love endures despite all our sin and rebellion because Christ has already paid for it.

This picture of God's love hits home for the Corinthian believers because Paul has spent a lot of time telling these rebellious young Christians what they're doing wrong—their sexual sins are even worse than the pagans', they're arrogant and power-hungry, and they don't know God's Word. But as he's pointing those things out, Paul also makes sure to remind them of his love for them and God's love for them. Patient, kind, not arrogant or rude, enduring all our sins—these are all the things God is to us.

If your heart is off track, rest assured that God has not turned His back on you. He's here, reminding you that His love for you endures. If you've wandered off into sin, come back to Him today. He's where the joy is!

DAY 27

Love never ends. As for prophecies, they will pass away; as for tongues, they will cease; as for knowledge, it will pass away. We know in part and we prophesy in part, but when the perfect comes, the partial will pass away. When I was a child, I spoke like a child, I thought like a child, I reasoned like a child. When I became a man, I gave up childish ways.

1 CORINTHIANS 13:8–11

Paul is writing to the Christians in Corinth, who deeply desire to be spiritually powerful. They want to prophesy and speak in other languages and show off all their so-called knowledge. Paul reminds them that all of the things they might know or do are temporary at best and meaningless at worst—especially if love isn't the motivating factor.

For instance, if they had the power to heal someone, that person would still die someday. Miracles are just a sign pointing us toward something else, something eternal. Paul wants these believers to mature in their faith and to see what those miraculous signs point to: God's great love is the point—His love, not our giftings. All the things we perceive to be our strengths will fail eventually.

If you feel like a failure today—always reaching for that perfect, future version of yourself who does powerful and impressive things so you can feel accepted by God and others—know this: God meets you in your imperfection, and He's not going anywhere. Joy isn't in becoming a better version of yourself. It's in Him. He's where the joy is!

THE GOD WHO GRANTS RIGHTEOUSNESS

2 CORINTHIANS 5:7–10

DAY 28

> We walk by faith, not by sight.
>
> **2 CORINTHIANS 5:7**

What an encouraging truth! The apostle Paul wrote this letter about a year after the last passage we covered—the famous "love chapter" from his first letter to the Corinthians.

In this section, Paul gives a nod to the great amount of suffering and confusion the Corinthian church is going through. Not only are they struggling, but they don't know which leaders can be trusted to guide them through it.

Maybe you can relate? Paul certainly can. In fact, he was nearly killed just before he wrote this letter. His words of truth still encourage us today: Our hope doesn't lie in our circumstances, and it doesn't rest on the trustworthiness of leaders. Our hope rests on the finished work of Christ, who has paid our sin debt and granted us His righteousness!

What circumstances are making it hard for you to trust God right now? What answers are you seeking from Him? Where you feel frustrated or fragile today, remind your heart that your eternity is secure and that God will handle all the details in His perfect timing. He's given you everything you need for life and godliness (2 Peter 1:3). He's where the joy is!

DAY 29

We are of good courage, and we would rather be away from the body and at home with the Lord. Whether we are at home or away, we make it our aim to please him.

2 CORINTHIANS 5:8–9

We are of good courage." Are you of good courage today? Do you find it easy to remember where your hope lies? Or does the world speak louder than the gospel?

As the apostle Paul writes these words to the church at Corinth, he's just on the other side of a lot of trials. In fact, in this letter he also says he recently despaired of life itself, thinking he'd been given a death sentence. But here he says that even when we do face death, we're entering into something far better.

Until that day comes, Paul focuses on pleasing the Lord. How do we please the Lord? Hebrews 11:6 says, "Without faith it is impossible to please [God]." Scripture repeatedly links our faith in God to our righteousness, but we don't earn one via the other—they're both granted to us by God! Faith is God's gift to us (Ephesians 2:8–9), and Christ's righteousness is "credited" to us (see Romans 4:22 NIV).

Be of good courage today. He rescued you from your sin. He triumphed over all your trials. He gives you all you need for life and godliness. In every moment, you're living as His beloved—a sinner reconciled to a Holy God. He's where the joy is!

DAY 30

We must all appear before the judgment seat of Christ, so that each one may receive what is due for what he has done in the body, whether good or evil.

2 CORINTHIANS 5:10

These words are part of Paul's second letter to the Christians in Corinth. Why would he say such jarring words to them—especially at a time when they likely needed encouragement?

This reminder might be timely for them. Remembering that our days are numbered helps us prioritize the eternal things and demonstrate our faith. On the contrary, the Corinthians are known for their sinful exploits. This warning may prompt them to recalibrate.

While the thought of God's judgment may be terrifying, this is where our hearts can find rest in the fact that our salvation isn't earned by our actions. Christ's righteousness is attributed to us, just as Paul says a few verses later: "In him we might become the righteousness of God" (5:21). We're declared righteous not because of our works but because of His. We could never live up to God's requirements for holiness and righteousness, but praise God, He does the doing!

Are you tempted to rely on your own good works to win God's approval? Do you ever try to impress God or worry that you've let Him down? What would it feel like to trust in Christ's righteousness today? He's where the joy is!

THE GOD OF ALL NATIONS

GALATIANS 3:1–9

DAY 31

O foolish Galatians! Who has bewitched you? It was before your eyes that Jesus Christ was publicly portrayed as crucified.

GALATIANS 3:1

Wow! Who is Paul calling a bewitched fool? That's strong language. This is Paul's letter to the churches in Galatia, a region near modern-day Turkey.

If you read the New Testament, you'll see a lot of conversations about the differences between Jews and Gentiles—*Gentile* is a collective term that refers to anyone who isn't a Jew. One of the major controversies in the first-century church surrounds the question of whether the Gentiles who follow Jesus have to start living like the Jews and following all 613 of the Old Testament laws.

When Paul writes this letter, it's roughly two decades after Jesus's death and resurrection. There are people alive who witnessed Him crying out from the cross, "It is finished" (John 19:30). Paul points them back to this moment as the foundation for the conversation about the law. He wants to remind them where their righteousness comes from and who their faith is in.

It's easy to move through our days as Christ followers and forget what He's done for us. Pause today and remember what He accomplished on your behalf—He paid your sin debt, assigned you His righteousness, and granted you the faith to believe! What a Savior! He's where the joy is!

DAY 32

Let me ask you only this: Did you receive the Spirit by works of the law or by hearing with faith? Are you so foolish? Having begun by the Spirit, are you now being perfected by the flesh?

GALATIANS 3:2–3

Many of the believers Paul is writing this letter to are of Gentile (non-Jewish) descent. They believe in the death and resurrection of Jesus, who, even though He's Jewish, offers salvation to people of all nationalities.

This concept is hard for both the Jews and Gentiles of Paul's day to grasp, so the church is wrestling with it. Jesus kept all the Jewish laws—not just the Ten Commandments, but all 613 of them. So their big question is whether the Gentile believers are required to follow the same laws as their Jewish Messiah and Jewish counterparts.

We have similar debates in the modern religious circles: *What is required of us?* What is your answer to that question? What is the foundation of the Christian faith? And what are some things you've heard others list as requirements or fundamentals that aren't?

Here, Paul gives them the best news imaginable: Jesus fulfilled those things *for us*. We're saved through faith in His perfect life of righteousness and His complete provision in His death—not by our own actions. What a generous God! He's where the joy is!

DAY 33

Did you suffer so many things in vain—if indeed it was in vain? Does he who supplies the Spirit to you and works miracles among you do so by works of the law, or by hearing with faith—just as Abraham "believed God, and it was counted to him as righteousness"? Know then that it is those of faith who are the sons of Abraham.

GALATIANS 3:4–7

The apostle Paul is in the middle of clarifying some of the fundamentals of the Christian faith for the new believers in Galatia. They're Gentiles who didn't grow up living by the Jewish laws, but now that they're following the Jewish Messiah, there's debate about whether they should start adhering to the law. Paul shares some incredibly good news with them: Their relationship with God isn't based on keeping the law.

God gave them His Holy Spirit before they ever obeyed any of the laws, before they ever started trying to live up to His standards. God didn't give them His Spirit because they were doing everything right. Paul reminds them that Abraham was counted righteous by his faith in God, and they are too.

Today, if you're burdened by all the ways you fall short, remember that God took all that into account, yet He still chose to adopt you into His family. No matter your heritage or nationality, if you have faith in God, you're a child of Abraham! And if your faith feels shaky, ask Him for more faith: "I believe; help my unbelief" (Mark 9:24). He stands ready to help you. He works miracles. And He's where the joy is!

DAY 34

The Scripture, foreseeing that God would justify the Gentiles by faith, preached the gospel beforehand to Abraham, saying, "In you shall all the nations be blessed." So then, those who are of faith are blessed along with Abraham, the man of faith.

GALATIANS 3:8–9

Throughout the Old Testament, God kept dropping hints and promises that He was going to send a Messiah to the Jews who would also be a bridge to reach the non-Jews, collectively referred to as Gentiles. Here, in this letter to the churches in Galatia, Paul references this and quotes one of God's promises from the Old Testament to prove that this has been God's plan all along: "In you [Abraham and his descendants] shall all the nations be blessed."

This idea of the gospel going out beyond the walls of the synagogues is not new—God's message of restoration and hope came through the Jews, but it was for *all* nations, not just the nation of Israel. As sinners born into a fallen world, we all started out as God's enemies, but our great God stepped over enemy lines to rescue us into His family.

Regardless of your nationality, you are a beloved child of God. Is that hard to believe? Do you find yourself trying to earn His favor through your actions? Today, remember what He promised long before you were born and how He accomplished it on your behalf! He's where the joy is!

THE GOD WHO PROTECTS US

DAY 35

Be strong in the Lord and in the strength of his might. Put on the whole armor of God, that you may be able to stand against the schemes of the devil.

EPHESIANS 6:10–11

Every day you face a battle. You're not only fighting the battle against your own sinful desires, but you also have unseen enemies who love to lie to you. Satan is scheming against you, actively working to steal, kill, and destroy all that God is doing in your life.

Satan wants to mislead you, and two of the primary ways he spreads lies are by tearing God down and by puffing you up. When he tempted Eve, he appealed to her flesh and entitlement, making her think God was cruelly holding out on her. His words sounded empowering, but they were lies, and she believed them, fracturing her relationship with God.

In today's passage, Paul reminds us that we don't walk in our own strength. He takes our gaze off ourselves and puts it on God. By remembering who God is, we can walk in His strength, not our own.

At some point in your life, you'll face more than you can handle. Maybe that's where you find yourself today. Despite what the catchy coffee mugs and social media posts say, you're *not* enough. But God is. And His power lives in you to strengthen you and protect you in whatever you face today. He's where the joy is!

DAY 36

We do not wrestle against flesh and blood, but against the rulers, against the authorities, against the cosmic powers over this present darkness, against the spiritual forces of evil in the heavenly places.

EPHESIANS 6:12

At a time when the early church has lots of visible enemies, Paul writes to the believers in Ephesus to remind them that there's even more going on behind the scenes. He doesn't tell them this to scare them but to *equip* them—because it's hard to win a battle against enemies we don't know exist.

In particular, this enemy launches attacks in our minds, lying to us and about us. The word *satan* is a common noun that means "the accuser." And according to this verse it seems there are *many* of these types of unseen forces working against God's kids. God's enemies love to accuse Him to us *and* to accuse us to ourselves. They want us to forget who He is, to doubt that He is good. But the truth of who God is acts as a protective device against the enemy's lies.

What lies are you tempted to believe about God? Today, preach the truth to yourself when the enemy lies to you. Remind yourself that God loves you, that He is for you, that He protects you from His enemies and works on your behalf even in the spaces you're unaware of. Remind yourself that He's where the joy is!

DAY 37

Take up the whole armor of God, that you may be able to withstand in the evil day, and having done all, to stand firm.

EPHESIANS 6:13

Because God knows you and He cares for you, He hasn't left you without help. He has made a way for you to face temptation, to stand firm against it, and to win—because, ultimately, it's a victory Christ has already won over all His enemies by His death and resurrection.

Jesus knows how hard it is to be human. He doesn't expect you to fight in your own strength. Not only does God offer the protection of His armor for the battles you face (we'll learn more about this armor in the days ahead), but His Spirit lives in you and empowers you in every moment. He never leaves you alone.

Where do you feel weak today? Where does it seem impossible to stand firm? Is it in a sinful pattern you can't seem to escape? A godly action you want to lean into but can't seem to find the desire or the strength? A troubling thought pattern you feel trapped in? He gives you all you need to stand firm. Ask for His help! He's with you, and He's where the joy is!

DAY 38

Stand therefore, having fastened on the belt of truth, and having put on the breastplate of righteousness, and, as shoes for your feet, having put on the readiness given by the gospel of peace.

EPHESIANS 6:14–15

Paul has been telling the Ephesians about their unseen enemies and the ways God has provided for their protection against those enemies. Here he offers up a helpful metaphor; he calls it the armor of God.

First, God give us the belt of truth. For soldiers, the belt is used to secure the breastplate in place *and* to hold their weapons. In spiritual terms, the truth is what secures our righteousness and it's also what upholds our weapon. The great truth Paul is referring to is the truth of the gospel and who God is—the very foundation of our faith.

The breastplate of righteousness reminds us that righteous living guards our hearts against the enemy's attacks. Paul also says to put on the shoes of the gospel of peace. What does that mean? The gospel is the good news that Jesus has granted us peace with God through His life and death. We can be ready to walk into every situation with our hearts at peace, proclaiming the gospel and trusting Him.

Do you find that you lack any of these things—truth, righteousness, or peace? Ask Him to help you suit up today! He's where the joy is!

DAY 39

In all circumstances take up the shield of faith, with which you can extinguish all the flaming darts of the evil one; and take the helmet of salvation, and the sword of the Spirit, which is the word of God, praying at all times in the Spirit, with all prayer and supplication. To that end, keep alert with all perseverance, making supplication for all the saints.

EPHESIANS 6:16–18

Paul's metaphor about the armor of God helps us understand how vigilantly God protects us. He gives us so many resources! When the enemy shoots his lies at us, we hold up our faith in Jesus as the response. And guess what? That shield of faith isn't a piece of armor we fashion on our own—it's a gift from God.

The helmet of salvation serves as our protective assurance that God has saved us, and the sword of the Spirit is God's Word. In all the armor listed, Scripture is the only piece that is an actual weapon used in offense. Everything else is for defense.

The last thing Paul mentions is prayer—for ourselves and for other believers. He reminds us that we need to ask for help through prayer, no matter what troubles we face. Talking to God is an act of protection in our war against the enemy. What battles are you facing today? Stop for a moment and talk to Him about them! He is your help in every battle you endure. He's where the joy is!

DAY 40

And [pray] also for me, that words may be given to me in opening my mouth boldly to proclaim the mystery of the gospel, for which I am an ambassador in chains, that I may declare it boldly, as I ought to speak.

EPHESIANS 6:19–20

Isn't this beautiful? The apostle Paul asks the church in Ephesus to pray for him. If he needs prayer, we certainly do too. He knows that prayer is part of our protection against the enemy's attacks.

One noteworthy thing about the armor of God is that all the major areas of vulnerability are protected, with the exception of one: the back. Soldiers compensate for this gap by standing back to back with each other. They have each other's backs.

Even though Paul writes this letter while he's in prison for preaching the gospel, he doesn't ask them to pray that he'll be released. Instead, his prayer request is for more opportunities and boldness in sharing the gospel—the very thing that landed him in prison. He doesn't want his trials to rob him of the opportunity or the zeal to talk about who Jesus is.

Do you have someone who will have your back in prayer? Do you pray for them regularly as well? And do your prayers echo the kind of values that Paul demonstrated—prioritizing the kingdom above all else? Today, fix your eyes on the eternal as you fight through the temporary. Fix your eyes on Jesus! He's where the joy is!

THE GOD WHO IS WORTH IT

PHILIPPIANS 3:7–11

— **DAY 41** —

Whatever gain I had, I counted as loss for the sake of Christ. Indeed, I count everything as loss because of the surpassing worth of knowing Christ Jesus my Lord.

PHILIPPIANS 3:7–8a

In the darkest moments of your life, what do you cling to? Paul writes these words to the Philippians while he's in prison, which is surely a challenging experience for him. Prisons at the time are a far cry from the more humane versions in the West today. Often, prisoners had to depend on outsiders to bring them food, medicine, and clothes.

Prior to this prison stint, Paul had been a respected leader in the community. He had power and honor. But now, after turning to follow Christ, he faces very real, life-threatening persecution. Have you ever lost something to follow Jesus? Maybe it meant walking away from a job to pursue God's calling on your life. Maybe it meant ending a relationship that wasn't God honoring. Maybe it was a sin pattern—one you hated or even one you loved.

Following Jesus will cost you something. But it will also give you something—the only thing—worth clinging to. Paul says it's more valuable that everything else! The joy of knowing Jesus not only far outweighs fleeting earthly pleasures but it also sustains us through life's harshest losses, because we *can't* lose Him—and He's where the joy is!

DAY 42

For his sake I have suffered the loss of all things and count them as rubbish, in order that I may gain Christ and be found in him.

PHILIPPIANS 3:8b–9a

To follow Christ, Paul walked away from his old life of power and prestige. But he didn't just lose his fame and become a regular person; as a result of following Jesus, he also lost his freedom and was thrown into prison. But as he looks back on his extreme losses, he considers those things rubbish. In the original Greek, *rubbish* would've been a curse word. That's how emphatic Paul is about the place earthly blessings hold in comparison to the eternal joys of a relationship with Jesus.

Earthly blessings aren't wrong or sinful—they're just not worth comparing to Jesus. Paul doesn't say they're second compared to Jesus—he says they're *rubbish* compared to Jesus. They aren't stable enough to hold your identity or your hope. They aren't valuable enough to build your life around. And on top of that, they're often a distraction from the one thing that *is* truly worth it.

Have you put your hope in the wrong things? Have they disappointed you? Surely you know that earthly joys are fleeting. The things we often value most have a way of letting us down. They fail and fade and fall apart. Nothing lasts except Him. He's where the joy is!

DAY 43

Not having a righteousness of my own that comes from the law, but that which comes through faith in Christ, the righteousness from God that depends on faith.

PHILIPPIANS 3:9b

Have you ever felt like you were failing at following Jesus? Have you despaired because you thought God was disappointed in you? If so, let these words from the apostle Paul set your heart at rest. This is the man who wrote two-thirds of the New Testament, much of it while imprisoned for preaching the gospel, and even he knows his righteousness isn't enough to please God.

Interestingly, this realization doesn't lead him to despair—it leads him to praise. His own attempts at righteous living may be honorable and wise, but they're worthless as efforts to earn God's favor. But, praise God, the righteousness of Jesus has been credited to his account. God has given him not only the faith to believe, but also the righteousness of Christ that is faith adjacent.

We're unworthy of God's blessings. But like Paul, we can delight in the great worthiness of Christ, who shares His blessings and inheritance with us. We were His enemies, children of wrath, but He adopted us into His family and made us His kids. Every good gift and action is from Him and points us back to Him. He's where the joy is!

DAY 44

> I want to know Christ—yes, to know the power of his resurrection and participation in his sufferings, becoming like him in his death, and so, somehow, attaining to the resurrection from the dead.
>
> **PHILIPPIANS 3:10–11** NIV

Paul is writing to the Philippian church from the confines of his prison cell. But instead of complaining about how he's been falsely accused and deserves to be set free, Paul seizes the opportunity to imitate Jesus. Jesus emptied Himself when He faced oppression. And Paul does too. He leans into humility.

In Matthew 16:24–25, Jesus said, "If anyone would come after me, let him deny himself and take up his cross and follow me. For whoever would save his life will lose it, but whoever loses his life for my sake will find it." Paul is living by those words.

Following Jesus will humble you. Life won't always go the way you want it to, and it will cost you something, but in the end, you will gain everything that matters, everything that is eternally valuable. You may lose temporary things—wealth, power, relationships—but you'll gain something that far outweighs it all as you're conformed to the image of Christ.

What has it cost you to follow Jesus? Is there something He's asking you to surrender to Him today? Ask Him to guide your steps as you take up your cross, and wait to see His resurrection power at work in your life. He's where the joy is!

THE GOD WHO IS PREEMINENT

COLOSSIANS 1:13–20

DAY 45

> He has delivered us from the domain of darkness and transferred us to the kingdom of his beloved Son, in whom we have redemption, the forgiveness of sins.
>
> **COLOSSIANS 1:13–14**

Today Paul gives us a little glimpse into our own stories. Did you know that you used to be in the domain of darkness? Scripture says we were born as enemies of God, children of wrath by our nature, living in darkness. Wow!

Because our hearts are naturally selfish and turned inward, there is no way we could've found our way to God in the darkness. But God knew our need, and His heart was set on rescue. He sent His Son, Jesus, to pay our enormous sin debt. He forgave us, redeemed us, and granted us new hearts turned toward Him.

Have you ever thought, *I'm a good person*, or *She's a good person*? In popular culture, one of the common refrains is this: People are basically good. But Scripture paints a different picture. It tells us the truth about who we are, and none of us gets a pass on needing a Savior. We cannot save ourselves, and we can't find our way out of the dark. Many people even love the dark more than the truth.

But Jesus, who is more powerful than the dark and greater than our hearts, has shown His preeminence over all things by redeeming us. He's where the joy is!

DAY 46

He is the image of the invisible God, the firstborn of all creation.

COLOSSIANS 1:15

Have you ever felt like God had a personality transplant between the Old Testament and the New Testament? It's a common misconception, and this verse sets us straight on that line of thought.

Here, Paul says Jesus is the image of the invisible God. So if you want to see what the Father's heart looks like—His personality and motives—look to Jesus. They are identical. As two-thirds of the Holy Trinity, the Father and Son have a shared nature. Jesus reveals the Father to us.

Paul also says Jesus is the firstborn of all creation. But that doesn't mean He was created. Jesus has always existed. In ancient Hebrew culture, calling Him the "firstborn" was a nod to His ranking. He has authority and preeminence over all created things.

Is there some area of your life that you haven't surrendered to His authority? Is there anything you're trying to hold back for yourself? Our good God can be trusted. His heart toward you is good. And as His sovereign plan to restore creation is being worked out in your life, you'll find your greatest joy in yielding to His authority. He's where the joy is!

DAY 47

> By him all things were created, in heaven and on earth, visible and invisible, whether thrones or dominions or rulers or authorities—all things were created through him and for him.
>
> **COLOSSIANS 1:16**

This section of Paul's letter to the church at Colossae is one the most succinct and densely packed descriptions of Jesus in the whole Bible. This is one of the verses (along with passages in John 1, Hebrews 1, and 1 Corinthians 8) that credits Jesus with the work of creation. Genesis 1 tells us the creation story, but verses like this take us deeper into that story.

The picture Scripture paints is one in which the Father gives the creation commands and the Son responds to those commands, fulfilling the manual labor of creation. God the Son created heaven and earth and every created being—human or otherwise. When He took on human form as a baby named Jesus, He stepped into the very physical realm He created in a personal, intimate way.

Paul says that not only was everything made through Him, but *for* Him as well. He is preeminent over all creation, and everything points back to Him. He made you, on purpose, for His glory. He delights in you. Do you believe it? And do you delight in Him too? Today, may your awareness of His affection help you delight in Him all the more, because He's where the joy is!

DAY 48

He is before all things, and in him all things hold together. He is the head of the body, the church. He is the beginning, the firstborn from the dead, that in everything he might be preeminent.

COLOSSIANS 1:17–18

Do you ever feel like everything in your life is coming unhinged? All your best-laid plans have failed, and you're waiting for the next disappointment or bit of bad news?

God sees your pain. He is not removed from it. In fact, He's the one holding you together right now. He goes before you in all things and is supreme over all things—that's part of what Scripture means when it says He is preeminent. But this doesn't mean you won't experience trials. It means your pain matters—it won't be wasted, and God will ultimately cause it to serve your greatest joy.

Scripture often refers to all believers as one body, and Christ is our head. Not only is He united to us, but He's also in charge. What a relief! I'm so glad I'm not in charge, that I don't have to determine my own path.

Jesus is also the beginning, the firstborn from the dead, which means He leads the way for us into the resurrection life. He has triumphed over death and has invited us to join Him as His resurrected coheirs in eternity. Count me in! He's where the joy is!

DAY 49

In him all the fullness of God was pleased to dwell, and through him to reconcile to himself all things, whether on earth or in heaven, making peace by the blood of his cross.

COLOSSIANS 1:19–20

In his letter to the church at Colossae, Paul pulls back the curtain on who we are and who Jesus is. These verses are saturated with awe-inspiring statements about Jesus, God the Son, the preeminent One.

In Him, we see all the fullness of God. Earlier in this section, Paul calls Jesus "the image of the invisible God." In other words, if you want to see what the Father's heart looks like, look to Jesus. They have a shared nature, character, and will. And God the Son, who is supreme over all things, condescended to earth in order to bridge the gap between God and man.

Bridging that gap required someone to exist in both spaces. Being 100 percent God and 100 percent man, Jesus is the only person who has ever filled that space. We're dependent on Him to connect us to the Father.

Are there broken relationships in your life that need to be reconciled? Ask God for help. He prioritizes reconciliation—reconciling us to Himself and reconciling us to each other in the scope of eternity. Jesus suffered great violence in order to achieve peace. His loss was our gain. What a Savior! He's where the joy is!

THE GOD WHO BUILDS HIS CHURCH

1 THESSALONIANS 5:12-18

DAY 50

> We ask you, brothers, to respect those who labor among you and are over you in the Lord and admonish you, and to esteem them very highly in love because of their work. Be at peace among yourselves.
>
> 1 THESSALONIANS 5:12-13

If you've been in church for any amount of time, you know that tensions can arise from almost any area at any given moment. Where humans are involved, things can always get sticky. In the apostle Paul's day, many of the churches are dealing with false teachers who need to be rejected and resisted. Paul does his fair share of that in some of his other letters.

However, the leaders of the church at Thessalonica are different; their leaders and teachers are godly and upright. Because Paul has personally endured the unique challenges of leadership, he knows the church leaders need to feel supported and encouraged, so he includes this in his letter.

Who are the spiritual leaders in your life? Have you ever taken the time to let them know you're praying for them and that you value them? One of the ways you can live out Paul's instructions to the church is by encouraging them—it has a way of promoting peace and sustaining them for the work God has called them to. May God use you to help build up His church. May your words remind them that their labor in the Lord isn't in vain, because He's where the joy is!

DAY 51

We urge you, brothers, admonish the idle, encourage the fainthearted, help the weak, be patient with them all.

1 THESSALONIANS 5:14

Have you ever been in charge of a group of people—a family, team, staff, or class? If so, you probably know what it's like to try to lead the group while the individual members are dealing with a wide range of emotions. This is true even of ourselves—our challenges can change just as often as our circumstances do. Maybe yesterday you felt lazy, today you're off the rails, and tomorrow you'll feel discouraged.

In this passage, Paul says each scenario requires a specific response, but they're all rooted in the gospel hope of Christ's finished work on the cross. Those who are idle need to be warned or rebuked with patience, those who are fainthearted need to be patiently encouraged, and those who are weak need our patient help.

Who needs your help in these areas today? You can be patient toward others because you've been in their shoes. At times, you've been idle, fainthearted, weak—and God was patient with you then, so you can extend His patience to others. He's at work in their lives to draw them near to Himself—and you may be one of the tools He uses to do that. What a gift to be used by Him to bless others and build His church! He's where the joy is!

DAY 52

See that no one repays anyone evil for evil, but always seek to do good to one another and to everyone.

1 THESSALONIANS 5:15

In his letter to the church at Thessalonica, Paul's words sound a lot like the Sermon on the Mount when Jesus said, "Love your enemies and pray for those who persecute you," and "As you wish that others would do to you, do so to them." When people sin against us, our natural response is to sin in return.

Sadly, this happens often within the context of church, because even though other Christians aren't our enemies, they're still sinners. If we aren't careful, we end up adding to the sin snowball and causing unnecessary division in the church. Paul and Jesus say we can live out a godly response instead. We can repay evil with good; we can repay cursing with the humble prayer that's a genuine blessing.

Who do you need to bless today? Who do you need to forgive? It's a hard calling, but Jesus did this very thing when He prayed for the men who crucified Him. His Spirit equips you with the patience required to bless your enemies—and even to bless those closest to you who have wounded you. His Spirit equips you to live out His words. As you follow in His footsteps, you'll see more and more that He's where the joy is!

DAY 53

Rejoice always, pray without ceasing, give thanks in all circumstances; for this is the will of God in Christ Jesus for you.

1 THESSALONIANS 5:16–18

Have you ever wondered what God's will for your life might be? There are a few places in Scripture where it's marked out plainly, and this passage is one of them. God's will for you is that you rejoice always, pray without ceasing, and give thanks in all circumstances.

How is this even possible? It's only possible for those who are in Christ. For Christians, *all* things—good, bad, and ugly—are being worked together by the loving hands of our Father for our ultimate joy and blessing. We can thank Him for working in all circumstances. We can take all our trials and desires to Him in prayer, and we can rejoice that He hears us, loves us, and is at work on our behalf.

Imagine a church full of Christ followers who lived like this! Imagine the trivial arguments that would disappear, the arrogance that would be humbled, the entitlement that would dissolve. If we lived this out, our lives and our churches would be places of peace and joy.

What's something you can rejoice about today? What can you pray about right now? What circumstance in your life can you thank Him for? Live out the will of God today. Rejoice because He's with you, and He's where the joy is!

THE GOD WHO EMPOWERS US

2 THESSALONIANS 1:11–12

We constantly pray for you, that our God may make you worthy of his calling, and that by his power he may bring to fruition your every desire for goodness and your every deed prompted by faith.

2 THESSALONIANS 1:11 NIV

Do you ever feel like you just can't do it all? There are so many standards to live up to, plus all the things on your to-do list, and you're falling short at every turn. If you feel like God has given you more than you can handle, you're right. But He hasn't given you more than *He* can handle.

God is the catalyst for all our good deeds, and He's the one who sustains us through them and for them. In Paul's second letter to the church at Thessalonica, he keeps reiterating this idea, showing us all the different ways it applies: God is the one who calls us. God is the one whose power is at work in us to make us bear fruit. God's character is the source and focus of our faith. *He does the doing.*

Where you fall short today, ask Him for help. He stands ready to help you. As you wait to see how things will play out, set your heart to trust Him for the outcome. He loves you, He's with you, and He's where the joy is!

DAY 55

[We pray] that the name of our Lord Jesus may be glorified in you, and you in him, according to the grace of our God and the Lord Jesus Christ.

2 THESSALONIANS 1:12

When you're in a relationship with someone, your actions reflect on them. And the closer the relationship, the truer this is. It's why we get embarrassed when our parents or children say something shocking on social media.

In his second letter to the Thessalonian Christians, Paul points to the relationship they have with Christ, and he prays that Jesus would be glorified in them. To give glory to God is to reveal Him rightly to the world around us—to show the weight and value of who He is. Do your actions point to His great worth? Do you talk about how lovable and praiseworthy He is? Or do your words and actions esteem other things as the biggest priorities in your life?

If you find that you're focusing more of your attention on fleeting things, ask God to help you prioritize Him and His kingdom above everything else. After all, that's exactly what Paul is doing in today's verse, so he's already set the example for us. God is the one who can change your heart. His love for you is what will empower your love for Him (1 John 4:19). He's where the joy is!

THE GOD WHO MEDIATES

1 TIMOTHY 2:1–6

DAY 56

I urge that supplications, prayers, intercessions, and thanksgivings be made for all people, for kings and all who are in high positions, that we may lead a peaceful and quiet life, godly and dignified in every way.

1 TIMOTHY 2:1–2

Here we find some of Paul's most challenging words in this letter. It's not always easy to pray for people in high positions, especially the ones who act unjustly or make decisions we disagree with. And it can be challenging to live a peaceful, quiet, dignified life, because we may want everyone to know our firmly held opinions. That's precisely why Paul had to write these words—*because* these things don't come naturally to us.

Paul is writing to Timothy, the young leader of a relatively new church in a pagan city where there are many false teachers. In the midst of their circumstances, Paul tells them to pray for those they oppose *and* to give thanks regardless. This posture results in an internal peace, even if it doesn't result in external peace.

This is what it looks like to trust God. It doesn't mean we don't take action against evil; it just means we can talk to Him in the process and leave the outcome up to Him. He sets our hearts at rest. Not only has Jesus acted as the mediator between us and the Father, but God acts as the mediator between us and our enemies as well. He's where the joy is!

DAY 57

This is good, and it is pleasing in the sight of God our Savior, who desires all people to be saved and to come to the knowledge of the truth.

1 TIMOTHY 2:3–4

We all want to please God, right? So what is it that Paul is calling good and pleasing in God's sight? If we zoom out to look at the verses prior to this, we see Paul urging the church to pray for those in political authority over them while leading a peaceful, quiet, godly, dignified life.

The church today could probably benefit from Paul's counsel to Timothy. God is pleased and honored when we live with wisdom and humility. And a beautiful side effect is that we don't obstruct the gospel with our arrogance. The gospel must go everywhere, even to those we oppose or disagree with.

Is there anyone you're too angry with or wounded by to pray for? Is there anyone you hope does *not* repent and come to know God? If so, that signals a need to check your heart for pride, bitterness, or resentment. The apostle Paul knows this personally—he was an anti-Christian terrorist before God saved him.

Jesus acted as the mediator between sinful man and holy God, and none of us deserve His rescue, but He extends salvation to sinners regardless. May we humble ourselves today. Aim to spread the peace and truth of His love to everyone you encounter. He's where the joy is!

DAY 58

There is one God, and there is one mediator between God and men, the man Christ Jesus, who gave himself as a ransom for all.

1 TIMOTHY 2:5–6

Have you ever tried to talk to someone who doesn't speak your language? The only way to truly communicate with them is to use a translator—someone who can speak both languages to bridge the gap. That's sort of what it's like in our relationship with God. We speak the language of fallen humanity. God speaks the language of holiness and deity.

Because He loves us, He planned all along to send a mediator: Jesus Christ, fully God and fully man, who is fluent in both languages, so to speak. Jesus bridged the gap so that anyone who wants to be in relationship with the Father can know Him, speak to Him, and be adopted into His family.

When we fail to rely on Jesus to bridge that gap, we'll often find ourselves clamoring to make our own strides. We try to impress God with our good behavior or earn His favor through checking all the right boxes.

But since Jesus has already accomplished all the Father requires of us, we're free to just obey Him out of love, to enjoy the peace of walking closely with Him! Praise be to God the Son, our mediator and our ransom. He's where the joy is!

THE GOD OF PATIENCE

DAY 59

All Scripture is breathed out by God and profitable for teaching, for reproof, for correction, and for training in righteousness, that the man of God may be complete, equipped for every good work.

2 TIMOTHY 3:16–17

One of the roles of Scripture is to equip us for every good work. It's the tool God uses to move us toward sanctification and completion, as only He can do. God's Word is His chosen means for this process, and He is the One who wrote it. He uses it to speak to us, guide us, and correct us as He reveals Himself to us.

He knows it will take us time to get to know Him and understand Him. Reading the whole Bible is arguably the best starting point for that. But make no mistake: It's not a box to check; it's air to breathe. It reveals the living God!

Have you read the whole Bible? You can read it in a year by reading for roughly twelve minutes a day. If you're a slow reader, there are apps and websites that read it aloud! Getting to know Him is a process, but He's patient with us as we try and fail and try again.

Start today. Scripture is the most trusted way God reveals Himself. He has beautiful things to reveal to you about who He is. And those things will change your heart forever in the most beautiful ways, because He's where the joy is!

DAY 60

I charge you in the presence of God and of Christ Jesus, who is to judge the living and the dead, and by his appearing and his kingdom: preach the word; be ready in season and out of season; reprove, rebuke, and exhort, with complete patience and teaching.

2 TIMOTHY 4:1–2

In Paul's second letter to his mentee, Timothy, he challenges him to preach God's Word at all times and to be prepared to patiently guide, correct, and encourage people. It can be challenging to teach or correct people—especially if you're conflict-avoidant—but the hardest part of this charge is probably the call for patience in the process.

As a young leader of a church in a pagan city, Timothy probably has to do a lot of correcting and rebuking, so it's vital for him to display that kind of patience. As Christians, we have access to patience because the Spirit of God lives in us and patience is one of His attributes. So Timothy can tap into God's kindness to *him* as he deals with others.

In the verses immediately before these, Paul says God teaches, reproves, and corrects us too. He has been patient with you. He continues to be. He delights in you and continues to extend kindness to you as you learn and grow. Those things He pours out to you are things you can extend to others you encounter today. He's where the patience is, and He's where the joy is!

DAY 61

The time is coming when people will not endure sound teaching, but having itching ears they will accumulate for themselves teachers to suit their own passions, and will turn away from listening to the truth and wander off into myths. . . . Always be sober-minded, endure suffering, do the work of an evangelist, fulfill your ministry.

2 TIMOTHY 4:3–5

False teachers tend to peddle one of two types of messages: *abundance* or *fear*. The abundance type ignores the message that Christians will suffer. The fear type ignores the message that, while suffering is promised, it isn't the point and it isn't the end.

Both of those things—abundance and fear—fix our eyes on the temporary, not the eternal, making it easy for us to be misled. Which are you most inclined to believe or think about? Which myths are most likely to draw you in? How do these verses help you recalibrate your thoughts to align them with the truth?

Timothy is the young leader of a church in a pagan city, and Paul reminds him to be sober minded—to be logical and sensible, not hot-headed or arrogant. He also encourages Timothy to endure suffering. After all, suffering is promised to us as Christ followers. In the meantime, Paul says the focus shouldn't be on resisting our opponents or on suffering, but on preaching the good news of Jesus.

What lies have distracted you from your mission? God patiently walks with you, leading you back to the truth. He equips you with all you need to show His love and truth to the lost world around you. He's where the joy is!

THE GOD WHO FULFILLS

TITUS 3:4–11

DAY 62

When the goodness and loving kindness of God our Savior appeared, he saved us, not because of works done by us in righteousness, but according to his own mercy, by the washing of regeneration and renewal of the Holy Spirit.

TITUS 3:4–5

Read through those verses one more time and try to locate all the words that point to God and His character and actions. *Goodness. Loving kindness. Savior. Mercy. Washing. Regeneration. Renewal.*

In addition to seeing these attributes, we also see all three persons of the Trinity represented here: Father, Son, and Spirit. The Father sent the Son to save us, and He also sent the Spirit to bring us to new life and continue His work in us. This was all set in motion by the Father's very good plan—and what He initiates He will sustain and He will fulfill.

Paul writes these encouraging words to a young pastor named Titus, whose church is struggling with false teachers. Titus may fear what could happen with the new believers, but Paul reminds him that God is the One who is building His church. God always finishes what He starts—and here specifically, as it pertains to salvation.

Have you ever doubted your relationship with God? Ever feared you've lost your salvation or wondered if you're really His child? Look back at the verse above one more time. Remember how He saved you. He gave you new life, and He isn't giving up on you. He's where the joy is!

DAY 65

Avoid foolish controversies, genealogies, dissensions, and quarrels about the law, for they are unprofitable and worthless. As for a person who stirs up division, after warning him once and then twice, have nothing more to do with him, knowing that such a person is warped and sinful; he is self-condemned.

TITUS 3:9–11

Titus is dealing with divisions in the church, and Paul knows how important it is for Titus to respond wisely. Paul doesn't just want his mentee Titus to be *right*, he wants him to be *wise*.

Paul says to avoid foolish controversies. Don't waste time on quarrels about the law; they don't benefit people. *But isn't truth important?* Yes, the truth of the gospel is important. But that's not what these quarrels in Titus's church are about—they're about second-tier and third-tier issues. When we get worked up over those things and we're willing to die on every hill, we lose our audience. They stop listening. They can't hear the gospel because we've shouted too long about other things.

If you were to divide your beliefs into three segments— absolutes, convictions, and opinions—what things would fall into each category? Are you able to articulate which things are fundamental to your faith? Are you able to let lesser things go when you're talking to Christians who have different convictions or opinions? Can you trust that God will work in their hearts (and yours) at the right time? He fulfills all He has planned!

Today, may you be an ambassador of peace, demonstrating God's love to the church and to the world. He's where the joy is!

THE GOD OF ALL JOY

DAY 66

I thank my God always when I remember you in my prayers, because I hear of your love and of the faith that you have toward the Lord Jesus and for all the saints.

PHILEMON 1:4–5

This is just the introduction to Paul's letter to a man named Philemon, but somehow Paul manages to fill it with theology. Even his hellos and good-byes can show us a lot about who God is if we pay attention.

So what do we see about God in these verses? Did you see who Paul thanked for Philemon's faith and love? Not Philemon. Instead, he thanks God for it. He rightly recognizes God as the source of all Philemon's faith and love and good works. God is the source, supply, and goal.

When we try to do things in our own strength, we will come to the end of ourselves. When we love and serve out of a vacuum, rather than out of an overflow, we may even begin to nurture frustration or anger toward those we serve. But when we tap into the love God has poured out to us, we're able to extend it to others.

Is there a relationship or role in your life where you're relying on your own strength? Ask God to equip you for it. Today, tap into the endless love He has for you so that you can serve with joy! He's where the joy is!

DAY 67

I pray that the sharing of your faith may become effective for the full knowledge of every good thing that is in us for the sake of Christ.

PHILEMON 1:6

Philemon is part of the first-century church, likely in Colossae. The church may have even met in his home. Paul writes to him from prison in Rome and begins the letter by talking about all the ways he's seen God working in Philemon's life.

Philemon has already been demonstrating God's love toward others in the church. Throughout the letter it becomes clear that he shares his faith in God with those around him, he loves and serves others, he forgives those who have sinned against him, and he points to the saving power of Christ.

Through all these actions, he reveals God's heart and character to those around him. Philemon's words and life demonstrate what it looks like to know God and be changed by Him. When others see that, God is glorified. These good things about Philemon point not to Philemon but to God! The point of his good works is to share Christ and *His* goodness!

Does your life make others curious about who Jesus is? Do you display your faith in word and in action? Do you have joy in trials? As the world watches, may you be the person God uses to reveal His heart. May your faith be effective in helping others see and know Christ. He's where the joy is!

DAY 68

I have derived much joy and comfort from your love, my brother, because the hearts of the saints have been refreshed through you.

PHILEMON 1:7

Have you ever been around someone whose presence made you feel refreshed and comforted? Someone who left you with reminders of God's love and joy? Paul writes this letter to Philemon, thanking him for being a person like this. From the darkness of his Roman prison cell, Paul remembers the light Philemon carries.

Philemon is known for demonstrating God's heart toward others in the church. Who has been that person for you? Who has pointed you toward the love and joy of Christ? Today is a good day to thank God for them and to let them know how He used them in your life.

Today is also a good day to take hold of the joy of the Lord for yourself so you can share it with others. As Christians, we should be known by this kind of love for others (John 13:35). We should be conduits of His joy, spreading it to everyone around us.

Who do you know that needs refreshing today? Who needs comforting? If God brought someone to mind, this is your chance to demonstrate His love to them. Even as Christ followers, we need to be reminded of His great love on a daily basis. He's where the joy is!

THE GOD OF OUR INHERITANCE

HEBREWS 1:1–8

DAY 69

Long ago, at many times and in many ways, God spoke to our fathers by the prophets, but in these last days he has spoken to us by his Son, whom he appointed the heir of all things, through whom also he created the world.

HEBREWS 1:1–2

Jesus has always had a special relationship with creation. As God the Son, He has always existed. The author of Hebrews says He came to dwell on the earth He created. And not only did He complete the manual labor of creation, but He will inherit it all as well. The Father appointed Him as the heir of all things.

According to Romans 8:16–17, we are His coheirs: "We are children of God, and if children, then heirs—heirs of God and fellow heirs with Christ." He built it, lived in it, inherits it, and shares it with all of God's adopted children forever.

In addition to that, He's one of the means by which God speaks to us, which is fitting because the apostle John calls Jesus "the Word" (John 1:14). From before the beginning of time, God planned to build this earth, redeem and restore it, and give it to His children as an inheritance. He's so generous!

Where do you see God's generosity in your life? Remembering His past and future kindness to us can help us trust Him in the present. If your eyes are focused on what you lack, train your heart to remember all He has given you and to thank Him for it! He's where the joy is!

DAY 70

He is the radiance of the glory of God and the exact imprint of his nature, and he upholds the universe by the word of his power. After making purification for sins, he sat down at the right hand of the Majesty on high, having become as much superior to angels as the name he has inherited is more excellent than theirs.

HEBREWS 1:3–4

This beautiful truth about Jesus is foundational to our faith. The author of Hebrews packs his letter with such rich descriptions that it's easy to skim over the poetic parts without digging into what they reveal on a deeper level.

What does it mean that Jesus is the radiance of the glory of God? It means He is the outgoing demonstration for the world to see the magnitude of who God the Father is. What does it mean that Jesus is the exact imprint of the Father's nature? It means they share the same character, personality, and will. God the Son shows us what God the Father is like. What does it mean that He upholds the universe? It means that not only did He create it, but He sustains it as well. He's intimately involved in all that happens here.

The author of Hebrews also compares Jesus with angels. But it's not a one-to-one comparison by any means. Jesus is far superior to the angels. *Angel* means "messenger," and while it's great to be God's messengers, Jesus *is* God. Jesus made the angels. They serve His purposes.

Which of these truths about Jesus is most comforting to you today? His goodness helps our hearts hold fast to Him as we await His return. He's where the joy is!

DAY 71

For to which of the angels did God ever say, "You are my Son, today I have begotten you"? Or again, "I will be to him a father, and he shall be to me a son"? And again, when he brings the firstborn into the world, he says, "Let all God's angels worship him." Of the angels he says, "He makes his angels winds, and his ministers a flame of fire." But of the Son he says, "Your throne, O God, is forever and ever, the scepter of uprightness is the scepter of your kingdom."

HEBREWS 1:5–8

Angels are intriguing and mysterious, aren't they? Fortunately, Scripture reveals quite a bit about them.

For instance, in this passage, we see that God doesn't command the angels to be worshipped, but instead commands the angels to worship His Son. In fact, the few times in Scripture when people mistakenly try to worship God's angels, the people are rebuked and reminded that God alone deserves our worship and praise. Angels are God's messengers. Jesus, however, is God the Son, the eternal King who reigns forever. His kingdom will never end.

Later in this chapter, the author also tells us that angels are sent to serve us. It's clear in Scripture that they are an entirely different type of created being; as humans, we don't become angels when we die. We were made in God's image, and like God the Son, we will live in our glorified resurrection bodies when we inherit the earth alongside Him!

What a comfort! The God who made the universe and who is praised by angels sits holy and sovereign over every moment of your life, loving you. And He promises that someday you, as His child, will reign with Him in His kingdom (2 Timothy 2:12). He's where the joy is!

THE GOD OF WISDOM

DAY 72

Who is wise and understanding among you? By his good conduct let him show his works in the meekness of wisdom.

JAMES 3:13

The book of James was almost certainly written by Jesus's brother. But interestingly, his name wasn't James. The original language reveals that his name was actually Jacob, but there was a discrepancy in the making of some of the early English versions and the mistranslation stuck.

For most of His life, Jesus's brothers didn't believe that He was the Messiah. Jesus's family members even mocked Him to His face (John 7:2–5). They didn't believe Jesus—*until* He resurrected from the dead. That'll do it!

Years later, James wrote these words to the Jewish members of the early church, encouraging them to walk in meekness and honor. James hadn't always done that, so he's speaking from the opposite experience when he gives this encouragement. He's grown in wisdom. He's been humbled. He demonstrates his wisdom and humility throughout this letter; he even opens by calling himself "a servant . . . of the Lord Jesus Christ"—from mocking Jesus to serving Him!

Knowing who Jesus truly is has a way of humbling us. Is there an area of your life where you need to humble yourself and walk in wisdom? Maybe you even need to go to someone and apologize for something you said in the past. May we walk in humble wisdom, and may Jesus be exalted. He's where the joy is!

DAY 73

If you have bitter jealousy and selfish ambition in your hearts, do not boast and be false to the truth. This is not the wisdom that comes down from above, but is earthly, unspiritual, demonic.

JAMES 3:14–15

As James continues to point us toward wisdom, he connects it to God. God is the source of true wisdom, and God's wisdom points us toward unity with other believers. Anything less than God's wisdom leaves us focused on ourselves, driven by our flesh.

How can you know when you're being driven by the flesh—when your sinful desires are ruling over your godly desires? One way you can tell is when you find yourself leaning into jealousy or comparison or pushing your own agenda. Sometimes that can even lead a person to distort the truth.

When Jesus's brother wrote these words to the early church, they were enduring lots of issues, both inside and outside the church. He wanted them to be united, not divided. One of the quickest ways the enemy can move us toward external division is by getting us to focus on our internal desires. We begin to withdraw from those who refuse to serve our purposes. We pressure and manipulate.

Where do you see earthly desires at work within you? Ask God for help to put those to death! Ask Him to grant you wisdom. Where do you see godly desires at work within you? Praise Him for it and live it out! He's where the joy is!

DAY 74

For where jealousy and selfish ambition exist, there will be disorder and every vile practice. But the wisdom from above is first pure, then peaceable, gentle, open to reason, full of mercy and good fruits, impartial and sincere.

JAMES 3:16–17

Wow! This passage is worth evaluating our hearts against. Do a careful search of your life and your relationships. Wherever disorder exists in your life, you'll probably find jealousy or selfish ambition at the root. Where you have vile practices—living in ways that are immoral or disagreeable—you'll find that you're lacking wisdom.

For instance, is your life chaotic because you're trying to keep up with the people you follow on social media? Are you walking in sin because you're guided by worldly principles and values instead of God's wisdom?

Scripture offers us a better truth, and the Spirit equips us to do it: Seek out the wisdom from above. Read the traits of God's wisdom again and ask the Spirit for help where you need it.

His wisdom is pure. It is peaceable. It is gentle. It isn't irrational—it can be reasoned with. It is full of mercy. It is full of good fruits. It is impartial. It is genuine. *This* is Jesus, and His Spirit lives in you to equip you to be and do these things as well! You'll find your greatest, deepest joy in imitating Him and walking in His wisdom, because He's where the joy is!

DAY 75

A harvest of righteousness is sown in peace by those who make peace.

JAMES 3:18

Did you know there's a difference between being a peace*maker* and being a peace*keeper*? Peacekeepers are driven by fear of man. They avoid conflict. They may turn their frustration into gossip or vent to others who can do nothing to actually help solve the problem. Sometimes they may keep things bottled up for so long that they explode. Peacekeeping is self-protective and doesn't serve the body of Christ.

Scripture never calls us to be peacekeepers. It calls us to be peacemakers—to enter into the chaos, bringing truth, hope, and love with us—and, through the patient work of the Holy Spirit, create peace where it didn't previously exist. This is a call to gentle courage, to persistent love.

When you're at odds with someone else or when you see others at odds with each other, what is your natural response? Do you stir the gossip and make things worse? Do you keep peace at all costs and avoid addressing the issue? Or do you enter into the chaos to bring the peace of God?

Peacemakers sow peace and wait for God to bring a harvest of righteousness. This is what wisdom looks like. God's wisdom is peace-adjacent. Today, may you plant peace everywhere you go. May your chaos-calming love remind those in conflict that He's where the joy is!

THE GOD OF FREEDOM

DAY 76

You are a chosen race, a royal priesthood, a holy nation, a people for his own possession, that you may proclaim the excellencies of him who called you out of darkness into his marvelous light.

1 PETER 2:9

What an incredible gift it is to be called *any* of these things! What's more astonishing is that Peter wrote these words to a church filled with believers who were mostly Gentiles, meaning they weren't Jewish.

For these non-Jews to be called chosen, royal, priests, holy, part of God's nation of people for His own possession—that is *huge*. It serves as a reminder that God wants freedom for people of *all* nations.

All these things are true of you too, Christian—chosen, royal, priest, holy, God's possession. It can be easy to read those words and imagine ourselves wearing the crown and the royal robes. But Peter quickly brings us back around to the point: *Because* we've been given those titles, and *because* God Himself has called us out of darkness and into His marvelous light, we should proclaim His excellence. These blessings and titles don't terminate on us; they point back to Him and His goodness!

As a person who has been rescued out of darkness, what aspect of your new identity and freedom are you most grateful for? Which of His "excellencies" can you praise Him for right now? Stop for a moment and praise Him! He's where the joy is!

DAY 77

Once you were not a people, but now you are God's people; once you had not received mercy, but now you have received mercy.

1 PETER 2:10

Have you ever been given an honor you knew you didn't deserve? Isn't it humbling? If that has ever happened to you, you may have felt like an imposter waiting to be found out. But God knows all the wrongs you've done and all the wrongs you've yet to do . . . and still, He chose to adopt you—His enemy by birth—into His family. You are one of His people, now and forever.

Ephesians 2 says we're all born as children of wrath, but here Peter says God's people have now received mercy—meaning God doesn't give His kids the punishment we deserve. We've earned the death penalty through our sin, rebellion, and brokenness. But because of His great mercy, we don't have to live afraid of His wrath.

Instead, His mercy is yours, because of Christ. He has set you free from death and punishment. Do you believe it? Or do you fear His wrath? Today, remember that Christ absorbed *all* the Father's wrath toward your sins when He died on the cross. There is no more wrath for you. You are free to draw near to the Father, who delights in you. He's where the joy is!

DAY 78

Beloved, I urge you as sojourners and exiles to abstain from the passions of the flesh, which wage war against your soul.

1 PETER 2:11

Have you ever felt like you didn't fit in? Like an exile or an outsider? In those instances, were you inclined to defend yourself or prove yourself? Did you give in to sins or desires you'd normally resist in order to gain social equity? What coping mechanisms did you cling to for help?

Peter is writing to Christians who live in a perverse society. It may be easy for them to want to gain social status or avoid trials. But Peter tells them to keep living as exiles and outcasts, not trying to fit in with the Romans. He says to abstain from the passions of the flesh—which include, but aren't limited to, things like vanity, gluttony, lying, sexual impropriety, slander, drunkenness, and greed.

These Christians are living under the rule of Rome, which is persecuting, taxing, and even killing them. They're facing a very real battle as a first-century church. But Peter spends his time highlighting an even bigger battle: the one our souls fight against our flesh. Peter knows what matters on an eternal scale.

What's waging war against your soul today? Where are you losing ground? Remember that He has granted you freedom from the power of sin. Walk with Him in the freedom He purchased for you! He's where the joy is!

DAY 79

Keep your conduct among the Gentiles honorable, so that when they speak against you as evildoers, they may see your good deeds and glorify God on the day of visitation.

1 PETER 2:12

You may really be able to relate to the Christians who got this letter from Peter. You may know what it's like to live among people who don't love God and think you're a terrible person for loving Him—maybe they're even people in your own home.

How does Peter tell the first-century Christians to handle situations like this? He doesn't say to make a list of all the reasons we're right and they're wrong and email it to them. He doesn't say to be passive-aggressive or act self-righteously. Instead, to these Christians whose very lives are at risk—not just their comfort—Peter says to conduct themselves honorably, to do good deeds that point to God. That's the way to catch the attention of those who persecute and criticize us, not by trying to prove them wrong.

When you're around others who disagree with you or who don't believe the gospel, how do you treat them? Are you more inclined to be rigid and harsh, focusing on proving your point? Or are you more likely to focus on living in ways that are honorable and upright? Does your life demonstrate the freedom and joy He has granted you?

Your actions represent God to those around you. Today, may you point to God with words and ways that are honorable and that glorify Him. He's where the joy is!

DAY 80

Be subject for the Lord's sake to every human institution, whether it be to the emperor as supreme, or to governors as sent by him to punish those who do evil and to praise those who do good.

1 PETER 2:13–14

These words are hard for us to hear today. No matter which political party you belong to—or even if you prefer not to affiliate with a particular party—at some point you'll be under the authority of someone you don't like or agree with.

Try to imagine what it was like for the Christians Peter wrote this letter to. Rome persecuted, taxed, and even killed them—yet Peter says to trust God with it all. God is sovereign over all authorities and all the moving parts of how they interact with their people.

While these verses remind us that the officials' role is to punish evil and praise those who do good, the reality is that our world is broken, so they won't always live out their roles perfectly. Some simply don't have the skills needed for leadership, and others are bent on acting wickedly.

So how can we trust God in these scenarios? Someday our King will set right all that has gone wrong in every human institution. Someday the internal freedom from sin's power that He has granted us will also be an external freedom from the sins of every oppressive, wicked leader. He's our eternal, righteous King, and we are subject to *Him* above all. He's where the joy is!

DAY 81

This is the will of God, that by doing good you should put to silence the ignorance of foolish people.

1 PETER 2:15

Have you ever wondered what God's will is? Have you ever flipped through your Bible trying to find it written out for you somewhere? Today, we're encountering one of the few places in Scripture where God's will is stated outright.

So what is it? This is His will: When foolish people act ignorantly, we should do good. His will is to use our good deeds—not our good rebuttals—to silence the fools. This type of response may seem counterintuitive, but it's not unlike God to give unexpected counsel that may feel a little too gentle (e.g., turn the other cheek, love your enemies, pray for those who persecute you, etc.).

Scripture talks a lot about how we use our mouths, and even though the internet didn't exist in the first century, I imagine this applies to the words we type with our fingers too. How do you respond to ignorance and foolishness when you encounter it—whether it's on the highway or on the internet or in a real-life interaction? Do you get angry, call people names, or maybe even roll your eyes? Or do you aim to keep doing good—even to them?

Today may your actions and words, and even the words you withhold, demonstrate the freedom you've found in Jesus. He's where the joy is!

DAY 82

Live as people who are free, not using your freedom as a cover-up for evil, but living as servants of God.

1 PETER 2:16

Peter wrote these words to a church living under Roman authority. They weren't free in the political sense, but they were free in the eternal sense—free from the power of sin to control them, free from the penalty of their sins because Christ had paid that debt for them. They were free in every way that mattered eternally.

However, Peter warned them not to exploit their freedoms or use them selfishly. Freedom in Christ isn't freedom to sin. It's freedom *from* sin. Freedom in Christ should never be confused with your right to be inconsiderate to others or unloving toward your neighbor. It's not an excuse to live however we want. We aren't the gods of our own lives; we've yielded to Christ as our Lord and Master.

Freedom in Christ means you're free from the bondage of your own selfishness. It means you're free to love your enemies, just like Jesus did. You're free of yourself, and you're a servant of God instead.

Does your life speak to this freedom? Where do you still live as though you're in bondage to sin? Where has your flesh enticed you back into your old prison cell? Drop your chains today, Christian! Christ has purchased your freedom from sin. Walk in holiness with Him—He's where the joy is!

THE GOD OF GRACE

DAY 83

May grace and peace be multiplied to you in the knowledge of God and of Jesus our Lord.

2 PETER 1:2

Not long before he died, Peter wrote this letter—probably from prison in Rome—to Christians who were facing persecution and possibly even martyrdom. In the introduction to his letter, he points us to one of the themes he repeatedly addresses: the ways God's grace shows up in our lives.

In biblical terms, grace is when God blesses us with something we don't deserve. In modern times, the word is often conflated with forgiveness or acquittal, and people use it to signal that we aren't held responsible for our sins. Grace is often confused with mercy, which is when God doesn't give us the punishment we deserve. However, grace is altogether different.

Grace isn't an excuse to sin. Grace is forward moving—it's God's work in our lives as an agent of change, calling us beyond where we are. It equips us to grow. Charles Spurgeon said it this way: "Grace is the mother and nurse of holiness, and not the apologist of sin."*

Peter says the more we know God, the more we'll know His grace and feel His peace. Where do you lack peace today? Where do you need His grace to empower change in you? Draw near to know Him. He's where the joy is!

*Charles Spurgeon, "Evening: January 25," in *Morning and Evening* (London: Marshall Pickering, 1990).

DAY 84

His divine power has granted to us all things that pertain to life and godliness, through the knowledge of him who called us to his own glory and excellence, by which He has granted to us his precious and very great promises, so that through them you may become partakers of the divine nature, having escaped from the corruption that is in the world because of sinful desire.

2 PETER 1:3–4

Did you know that you have all you need to live a godly life? If you know Jesus, then you have His Spirit living in you, equipping you with everything you need to love and honor God. How comforting to know that we're not left to do this in our own strength. He does the doing—and He does it for His own glory and excellence.

By His divine nature, our sinful nature is being transformed day by day. And someday, when Jesus returns, we'll live in resurrection bodies like His and all His "precious and very great promises" will be fulfilled.

All of these gifts are things we don't deserve. All of this is evidence of His grace being poured out in our lives, multiplied to us. We could never earn these things. They are the exclusive blessings of being His kids, being adopted into His family through no effort of our own.

Today, think about the immense gift He's given you by calling you His child. Revel in the blessings of His gifts to you! And as you delight in Him, may your smile and your gentleness point others to Him as well. He's where the joy is!

THE GOD WHO SAVES

1 JOHN 3:16–22

DAY 85

> By this we know love, that he laid down his life for us,
> and we ought to lay down our lives for the brothers.
>
> **1 JOHN 3:16**

The apostle John is credited with writing this letter, and love is one of his primary themes. That comes as no surprise from the apostle who is said to have referred to himself as the disciple Jesus loved (John 13:23).

One way love reveals itself is in our willingness to in-convenience ourselves for those we love. If I'm not willing to lay down my *preferences* for someone else, I certainly wouldn't lay down my *life* for them. But that's exactly how Jesus revealed His love to us—by laying down His life in order to save us.

The reality is, His saving love will always supersede our love. His love isn't tainted by sin and selfishness. Because of His great love for the Father, Jesus laid down His own de-sires to fulfill the Father's plan. Because of His great love for us, God the Son laid down His life, paying the debt for our sins and bridging the gap between us and God the Father.

Who do you let inconvenience you? Who do you sac-rifice for? While you and I can't save anyone else, we can demonstrate the saving love that rescued us, because His Spirit lives in us, empowering us to love others well. He's where the joy is!

DAY 86

If anyone has the world's goods and sees his brother in need, yet closes his heart against him, how does God's love abide in him?

1 JOHN 3:17

In his first letter, John talks about what true faith in God looks like. He says it will always result in action. But our actions don't *contribute* to our salvation; they're the *result* of our salvation. God does the saving work, not us.

Once we've been adopted into God's family and given new hearts, His Spirit comes to dwell in us and He works in us to make us look like Jesus. That's where our good works come from—they're the fruit of the Spirit's presence in our lives (Galatians 5:22–23). By His power, we begin to demonstrate true love, joy, peace, patience, kindness, goodness, faithfulness, gentleness, and self-control in our relationships with God and others.

When Jesus saw people hurting or in need, He leaned in. He sees your pain too—and He leans in. He also sees the pain of those around you, and He leans in there too . . . and maybe He even does it *through you*. John calls us to these acts of love.

Who do you know who is in need right now? What surplus do you have that you could offer to someone lacking? Today, pour out the kindness and goodness of the God who saved you. Maybe you are the way someone else will see and believe that He's where the joy is!

DAY 87

Little children, let us not love in word or talk but in deed and in truth. By this we shall know that we are of the truth and reassure our heart before him; for whenever our heart condemns us, God is greater than our heart, and he knows everything.

1 JOHN 3:18–20

Most people believe 1 John was written by John the apostle, who referred to himself as the disciple Jesus loved. And because he knew and believed God's love for him, he was able to extend that love to others too, even when it was inconvenient. After all, he was the one Jesus appointed to care for Mary after His death.

Our actions reveal what our hearts love. What do your actions reveal about you? What would the people around you say that you love? Get honest with yourself about this. Are you showing God's love to others?

On the other hand, if you're caught in a sin cycle, you're tormented by ungodly desires, or your heart is condemning you and you feel like you're a bad representative for Jesus, John has some encouraging words for you: God already knows, and He's bigger than your heart. Rest in the words of Romans 8:1: "There is therefore now no condemnation for those who are in Christ Jesus." He has saved you from the penalty of your sins!

God knows every sin you've ever committed and every sin you haven't committed yet—and He says Jesus's death is sufficient to cover them all. For God's children, there is no shame in His presence. Only love and joy. Because He's where the joy is!

DAY 88

Beloved, if our heart does not condemn us, we have confidence before God; and whatever we ask we receive from him, because we keep his commandments and do what pleases him.

1 JOHN 3:21–22

Christian, God has saved you and adopted you into His family. You're His child forever now. When your heart is aligned with His and you approach the Father in prayer, you can do it without fear of condemnation. You can do it with full confidence that He'll say yes to everything you ask that lines up with His heart. He's here to bless you with His yes for everything that is best.

How remarkable is it that we can have confidence before God! Where does that kind of confidence come from? It doesn't come from our own worth or perfection, because we have none on our own.

It comes from the finished work of Jesus, who perfectly obeyed the Father's commands, who perfectly pleased the Father, who was the perfect sacrifice for your sins. All of His goodness was attributed to you. He saved you and made you His own!

And He has many more good things to give you in addition to your salvation. What will you ask Him for today? Whether His answer to you is yes, no, or maybe, commit to trust Him. He has good in store for you, today and always! He's where the joy is!

THE GOD WHO SEEKS OUR HEARTS

2 JOHN 1:6

DAY 89

This is love, that we walk according to his commandments; this is the commandment, just as you have heard from the beginning, so that you should walk in it.

2 JOHN 1:6

All through Scripture, God reminds His people that He isn't just after our obedience—He's after our hearts. When He has our hearts, everything else follows. That's what love does to us. It reorganizes our priorities and pushes out the things of lesser importance. Thomas Chalmers called this "the expulsive power of a new affection." What we love determines our course.

Once, when a group of people asked Jesus what God required of them, Jesus replied that the work of God is that they believe in the one He sent, meaning *Jesus Himself*. That's it: Believe the truth about Jesus. That's what God requires. Then, when the seed of that belief takes root in our hearts, it bears fruit in our lives.

We live what we believe, because our hearts and minds and actions are all bound up together, inextricably. That's why Jesus said we should love God with all our heart and soul and mind and strength. If you were to examine each of those four areas of your life carefully, which one would you say reveals your love for God the most? Which one reveals your love for Him the least? Why?

In all those spaces—heart, soul, mind, strength—may you love Him all the more today. He's where the joy is!

THE GOD OF ALL GOODNESS

3 JOHN 1:11

DAY 90

Beloved, do not imitate evil but imitate good. Whoever does good is from God; whoever does evil has not seen God.

3 JOHN 1:11

In John's third letter to the church, he reminds us of who God is and calls us to imitate God's actions and character. And John particularly takes care to highlight God's goodness here.

Once we have beheld God, fixed our eyes on Him, and yielded to Him as our Lord, our whole lives are transformed. He gives us new hearts, we find ourselves moving toward new desires, and we have a peace that somehow stands even in the midst of trials and chaos. Everything is new.

And because Jesus triumphed over sin and death, we are no longer enslaved to our sins. We can actually do good instead of evil. Before we knew God, we were held captive by our sin, but now we're slaves to righteousness instead. We can imitate God and His goodness by the power of His Spirit at work within us.

Today, walk in your freedom over sin. Imitate God and His goodness. And when you see His goodness show up in your life, thank Him for it! He's the one who is good to you *and* through you! He's where the joy is!

THE GOD WHO STEADIES US

JUDE 1:18-25

DAY 91

> They said to you, "In the last time there will be scoffers, following their own ungodly passions." It is these who cause divisions, worldly people, devoid of the Spirit.
>
> JUDE 1:18–19

Jude was almost certainly the son of Joseph and Mary, which means this letter was written by Jesus's half brother, who probably also went by the name Judah. Here he references the words of the apostles—they'd warned the early church about unbelievers who were causing division inside the church.

As we look at the world today, we certainly see division. When the division is between believers and unbelievers, it can be incredibly unsettling and frustrating. At other times, divisions may occur within the church itself, which has the potential to be even more confusing. Each side points to the other side, accusing them of not heeding Christ's words and not living out His priorities. It's messy, isn't it?

So how do we know what's true? We read His Word. All of it. Otherwise we may be misled by outsiders. Or we may accidentally take it out of context and twist it to fit our own desires.

Have you read His Word? All of it? If you haven't, start today. May His Spirit breathe life into you through His Word. His Word will steady you in this shaky world. May you feel more equipped to create unity, to be an ambassador of peace. May He protect you from being misled and keep you firmly in the truth! He's where the joy is!

DAY 92

You, beloved, building yourselves up in your most holy faith and praying in the Holy Spirit, keep yourselves in the love of God, waiting for the mercy of our Lord Jesus Christ that leads to eternal life.

JUDE 1:20–21

Psychologists say that having a specific long-range goal in mind helps you to stay the course as you move toward that goal. But if you aren't specific, you're unlikely to make progress. And while Scripture isn't a self-help book, the same principle applies: *Keep the end in mind.*

Jude exhorts his readers to do just that. He reminds them that they're waiting for eternal life. That's their specific long-range vision. In the meantime, he tells them what to do and how to do it. He calls believers to build themselves up in the faith and to strengthen their love for God, and he reminds them that these things are only possible through communication with God and having access to His Spirit.

On a practical level, how do you build and strengthen any relationship? By spending time with the person. Scripture and prayer are two ways we spend time with God. And His Spirit, who lives in believers, equips us with words to pray. God Himself enables us to grow in faith and love, ushering us into greater intimacy.

When our minds are chaotic, His voice steadies us. When our hearts are faltering, His Spirit steadies us. And as we grow, we continue to fix our eyes on the merciful return of Jesus and our eternal life with Him. He's where the joy is!

DAY 93

Have mercy on those who doubt; save others by snatching them out of the fire; to others show mercy with fear, hating even the garment stained by the flesh.

JUDE 1:22–23

Do you find it challenging to deal with people who doubt God and His Word? Or maybe *you* are the one who has trouble believing God and His Word? The good news for doubters is that God calls Christians to extend mercy to them. This means *God* has mercy on them. Mercy is when we don't get what we deserve. It's often displayed through acts of patience and compassion and kindness.

But Jude says sometimes our mercy can be severe, taking action to try to rescue people from judgment, standing firm against sin. God hates sin in part because He loves people—and sin is harmful to people. So it's merciful to call them out of sin and into joy.

Can you think of a time when God showed you mercy through compassion? Or through severe action? Have you ever had to demonstrate one or both of these kinds of mercy to someone else?

Sometimes it's hard to know which kind of mercy would be most helpful. But God knows what doubting hearts need, and He knows what sinning hearts need. He sets us back on our feet again where we've fallen over or simply fallen into a crumpled heap. He steadies us. In fact, He's steadying you right now. He's where the joy is!

DAY 94

Now to him who is able to keep you from stumbling and to present you blameless before the presence of his glory with great joy, to the only God, our Savior, through Jesus Christ our Lord, be glory, majesty, dominion, and authority, before all time and now and forever. Amen.

JUDE 1:24–25

Earlier in his letter, Jude encourages believers to keep themselves in the love of God, and here he circles back to remind them that it's ultimately God who keeps them. He does the doing.

He's not a hands-off kind of God. He is the one who keeps you from stumbling. He is the one who steadies you. Jesus presents you blameless before God. He's keeping you forever, Christian. God is moving you toward ultimate joy through the finished work of Christ our Savior and King.

Our heart-steadying, future-sealing God confirms that you are His. And He does all the work required to save and keep you. This kind of love should turn our hearts toward Him in praise, which is what Jude does next. He praises the God who has always existed and has always had authority over all creation. He is crowned with glory, majesty, dominion, and authority.

In other words, not only does He have power over everything, but He's royal and powerful and beautiful. Do you ever wrestle with the fact that God is in charge? These verses remind us that He's the kind of ruler you *want* to be in charge of things. What a magnificent Savior! He's where the joy is!

THE GOD WHO WILL RETURN FOR US

DAY 95

I saw a new heaven and a new earth, for the first heaven and the first earth had passed away, and the sea was no more.

REVELATION 21:1

The apostle John has been sent to a prison island called Patmos where he'll live out his final days. While there, he writes a letter to the early church telling them about the return of Jesus. His words still apply to us today as we continue to wait for Jesus to come back and renew all things, including heaven and earth.

Why would heaven need to be renewed? Likely because it was marred by the sin of the fallen angels. Earth is renewed too (like it was after the flood). But according to this passage, the new earth will have some different features; specifically, it won't have a sea. For most of the people of John's day, this likely comes as a relief. The sea is wild and unmanageable; most are terrified of it. So the absence of the sea likely signals peace in their minds.

How do you feel when you imagine the end of the world? Are you at peace? Or are you inclined toward fear? Yes, it'll be the end of life as we know it, but that's not a bad thing. It's not something to be afraid of. As followers of Jesus, it's something to look forward to. We'll be living under the reign of King Jesus, and He's where the joy is!

DAY 96

I saw the holy city, new Jerusalem, coming down out of heaven from God, prepared as a bride adorned for her husband.

REVELATION 21:2

Whether you're male or female, if you're part of God's universal church, then you're part of the bride of Christ. Through this imagery, Scripture reveals the kind of eternal intimacy we get to have with the God of the universe. He has united Himself to us forever, and He created earthly marriage to serve as a picture of that union.

Since before He created us, God has been in the process of making a way to dwell with us forever. Through the finished work of Christ on the cross, through the way His Spirit dwells in us, and eventually through setting up His dwelling place with us on the renewed earth, He continues to pursue us.

This verse points us toward our future home with Him in the new heavens and the new earth. When heaven and earth are renewed, they seem to merge into a space John calls the holy city, new Jerusalem. When this new Jerusalem descends from heaven to earth, we'll dwell with God in eternal intimacy.

What excites you most when you think of our literal heaven on earth? Besides seeing loved ones who are there, what else do you long for? Look forward to His coming today. Ask Him to return! Echo the words of the saints, "Come, Lord Jesus," because He's where the joy is!

DAY 97

I heard a loud voice from the throne saying, "Behold, the dwelling place of God is with man. He will dwell with them, and they will be his people, and God himself will be with them as their God."

REVELATION 21:3

Since before God created the earth, He has always been making a way to draw near to sinners like you and me. We see this all throughout Scripture.

For instance, He didn't stay in the garden of Eden after Adam and Eve left. He pursued them and their offspring. Then He set up a literal camp in the desert with sinners. Then He showed them where to build His temple so He could dwell in the midst of them in Jerusalem. When He sent them into exile, He left the temple and went into exile with them!

And now, God says, *we* are His temple, His dwelling place. The Spirit of God dwells in you, while also still dwelling in heaven. But it won't always be that way. Someday heaven will descend to earth and we'll celebrate our eternal union with God as His bride.

How does it feel to know that God never wants to be apart from you? Did you know that He isn't scared off by your sin? In fact, He keeps pursuing you when you sin, like He did with Adam and Eve. He isn't going anywhere. He's right there with you, right now. I'm so glad He never stops pursuing us, because He's where the joy is!

DAY 98

> He will wipe away every tear from their eyes, and death shall be no more, neither shall there be mourning, nor crying, nor pain anymore, for the former things have passed away.
>
> **REVELATION 21:4**

As you know, I close every devotional reading with "He's where the joy is." Maybe you know God and you still have deep pockets of sadness in your life, so perhaps my words seem impossible for you right now. *What joy?*

Someday our sadness will be erased. But in this life, sadness and joy can be mingled together. In fact, they often are. You can be sad. God is not dishonored. He weeps with you. And your sadness doesn't cancel out the joy you have access to because of Him.

As Paul said in 1 Thessalonians 4, *our grief isn't hopeless*. Someday our ultimate hope will be fulfilled. Someday our God will renew, restore, and re-create. And when He remakes things, He turns them into better versions of what they were. He made mankind good but not perfect—but someday He'll finish conforming us to the image of His Son, Jesus.

What sadness are you holding today? Tell Him about it. Feel His nearness as He aches with you. As today's verse says, "He will wipe away every tear from their eyes." He cares that you're hurting. Then ask Him to help you access His joy too. You can hold both, because He holds them with you. He's where the hope is, and He's where the joy is!

DAY 99

He who was seated on the throne said, "Behold, I am making all things new." Also he said, "Write this down, for these words are trustworthy and true."

REVELATION 21:5

What things need to be made new in your life? What things are broken that have been completely out of your control? What things have *you* broken? Have you lost hope that those things can still find resolution?

Our world is filled with wreckage and pain. Not only do others sin against us and wound us, but we sin against others too. We all do so much breaking, and part of our brokenness means we want to point the finger at others and all they're breaking. Sometimes it can all be so overwhelming. We can barely handle the losses in our own lives and then we turn on the news and see that pain is multiplied the world over.

Imagine a day when God reverses the curse, when all things are restored and set right, when heaven and earth are fused together as one and we worship our reigning King Jesus. God says He is making all things new. All things. And do you know where God is sitting when He says this? On His throne. This isn't a promise from someone who can't fulfill it—*He's the King of the universe!*

There is hope yet for all you've lost or broken. But I think even our fulfilled hopes will pale in the light of our King who is coming back for us! He's where the joy is!

DAY 100

He said to me, "It is done! I am the Alpha and the Omega, the beginning and the end. To the thirsty I will give from the spring of the water of life without payment. The one who conquers will have this heritage, and I will be his God and he will be my son."

REVELATION 21:6–7

As John closes out his letter and as Scripture comes to a close at the end of Revelation, we're reminded that God surrounds everything. He's the beginning and the end. Every moment that ever was or will be falls under His reign of love.

One of the ways He demonstrates His love most clearly is when He gives us the water of life—*eternal* life—without receiving payment. He *gives* it. Freely. If we had to pay for it, it wouldn't be a gift. What do we even have to give the God of the universe in return for the water of life anyway?

In the gospel of John, Jesus refers to Himself as the Living Water. We get Jesus free of charge. He rescues us and doesn't send an invoice. On the contrary, He sends a deposit—His Spirit. He comes to dwell in us—again, for free. We have nothing to offer Him in exchange for this great rescue. He pursues us to bless us, not to take from us.

When someone asked Martin Luther what he contributed to his salvation, he allegedly said, "Sin and resistance." Maybe you can relate? Yet God freely gives Jesus and His Spirit to us. Take a minute today to stop and thank Him for His free gift of salvation, for granting you eternal life with Him! He's where the joy is!

Acknowledgments

Tara-Leigh would like to thank the following people:

- The team at *The God Shot* radio show: Eva Royer, Tyler Cox

- The team at KCBI (Dallas, Texas): Joel Burke, Taylor Standridge, Matt Austin, Kelly Corday

- The team at KSBJ (Houston, Texas) and Hope on Demand: Joe Paulo, Shawn Farrington, Scott Belin

- The team at Way-Nation and Way-FM: Tim Dukes, Ron Harrell, Zach Boehm

- The team at Bethany House: Jeff Braun, Hannah Ahlfield, Andy McGuire, Stephanie Smith, Deirdre Close, Rebecca Schriner, Mycah Gavic

- Lisa Jackson and Alive Literary Agency

- My parents and family, Jacqueline Terrell, Olivia Ramsey, Meg Roe, Anne MacDonald

- D-Group International: Leaders, members, fellows, and pals

- The Bible Recap team and every member of our Patreon family

About the Author

Tara-Leigh Cobble's zeal for biblical literacy led her to create and develop an international network of Bible studies called D-Group (Discipleship Group) International. Every week, hundreds of men's and women's D-Groups meet in homes and churches around the world to study Scripture.

She also writes and hosts a daily podcast called *The Bible Recap*, designed to help listeners read and understand the Bible in a year. The podcast garnered over one hundred million downloads in its first three years, and more than twenty thousand churches around the world have joined their reading plan to know and love God better. It has been turned into a book published by Bethany House Publishers.

Tara-Leigh speaks to a wide variety of audiences, and she regularly leads teaching trips to Israel because she loves to watch others be awed by the story of Scripture through firsthand experience.

Her favorite things include sparkling water and days that are 72 degrees with 55 percent humidity, and she thinks every meal tastes better when eaten outside. She lives in a concrete box in the skies of Dallas, Texas, where she has no pets, children, or anything that might die if she forgets to feed it.

For more information about Tara-Leigh and her ministries, you can visit her online.

Websites:	Social media:
taraleighcobble.com	@taraleighcobble
thebiblerecap.com	@thebiblerecap
mydgroup.org	@mydgroup
israelux.com	@israeluxtours

More from
Tara-Leigh Cobble

This attractive deluxe edition of *The Bible Recap* features an imitation leather cover, a ribbon marker, and a striking two-color interior. This makes the perfect gift for holidays, celebrations, or simply encouraging someone in their faith.

The Bible Recap Deluxe

Tie your study together with *The Bible Recap Journal*, which offers writing prompts and uniquely organized space perfect for recording and tracking each day through the whole Bible.

The Bible Recap Journal

You May Also Like . . .

Dig deeper into the Word with *The Bible Recap Study Guide* with daily reflection and research questions specific to each day's reading and space to write your responses and notes.

The Bible Recap Study Guide

BETHANYHOUSE